Soothing Your Child's Pain

From Teething and Tummy Aches
to Acute Illnesses and Injuries —
How to Understand the Causes
and Ease the Hurt

Kenneth Gorfinkle, Ph.D.

CONTEMPORARY BOOKS

Library of Congress Cataloging-in-Publication Data

Gorfinkle, Kenneth.
    Soothing your child's pain : from teething and tummy aches to
acute illnesses and injuries—how to understand the causes and
ease the hurt / Kenneth Gorfinkle.
        p.   cm.
    ISBN 0-8442-3255-3
    1. Pain in children—Popular works.   I. Title.
RJ365.G67   1997
618.92—dc21   97-27955
                                                            CIP

Interior design by Amy Yu

Published by Contemporary Books
An imprint of NTC/Contemporary Publishing Company
4255 West Touhy Avenue, Lincolnwood (Chicago), Illinois 60646-1975 U.S.A.
Copyright © 1998 by Kenneth Gorfinkle, Ph.D.
Printed in the United States of America
International Standard Book Number: 0-8092-3255-3
17   16   15   14   13   12   11   10   9   8   7   6   5   4   3   2

THIS BOOK IS DEDICATED TO
THE HUNDREDS OF CHILDREN WHO HAVE ALLOWED ME
TO HELP THEM HEAL THEIR PAIN.

Contents

Acknowledgments

A number of people guided my professional career toward caring for the medically ill and people suffering from pain. Without their encouragement over the past several years, this book could not have been written. At the Veterans Hospital in Manhattan in 1983, David Ruhland introduced me to the field of behavioral medicine and taught me basic skills in caring for U.S. veterans with chronic pain syndrome. At Memorial Sloan-Kettering Cancer Center in New York, Bill Redd, Paul Jacobsen, and Sharon Manne opened my eyes to the necessity of alleviating pain and suffering in children with cancer.

Thank you to Dee Jones, Tom Moulton, Lenny Wechsler, Kara Kelly, and Michael Wiener of the Department of Pediatric Oncology at Babies and Children's Hospital and especially to Penny Buschman Gemma, Jim Garvin, and Ria Hawks for their strong advocacy for the care of children's pain.

Thanks to Boris Rubenstein and Jonathan Slater for bringing me aboard the Child Consultation/Liaison Psychiatry Service, where I am confronted with and challenged by some of the most unusual and difficult pain problems afflicting children.

Much of my work at Babies and Children's Hospital and Columbia-Presbyterian was made possible by the generous support of the Nathaniel Wharton Fund, the Henry van Ameringen Foundation, and the Art Works Project.

I wish to acknowledge the ongoing support of the Behavioral Medicine Program at Columbia University, specifically Ethan Gorenstein, Richard Sloan, Kenneth Frank, Kenneth Greenspan, Dan Seidman, and Don Kornfeld. They allowed me to carve out the necessary time to get this book to print. They have been my strongest cheering section.

Thank you very much to Kara Leverte, my editor at Contemporary Books. Her suggestions and ideas came from her heart and from her life experience mothering her own little ones. Her intuition about what the book needed to aid mothers and fathers everywhere was tremendously helpful.

Many thanks to Ron Taffel, Michael Levi, and Carole Wolfe Korngold and K. T. Korngold for reading and making thoughtful comments on the emerging manuscript.

A special thanks to Loretta Barrett, my literary agent, who "discovered" me while I was giving a lecture on pediatric pain. It was Loretta's vision, her personal investment in carrying the idea to fruition, and her ongoing coaching of this neophyte writer that kept me inspired to write and write.

Finally, I thank Doris Ullendorff, my wife, mother of our children, and a great kisser of boo-boos for her ideas, anecdotes, thoughtful criticism, and her love. She keeps me going even when times get tough.

Introduction

Pain is pain! Whether from physical or emotional
causes, it hurts just the same. To deny this is to
forgo the feel of the soothing hand, a mother's
kiss—to alleviate and to heal.

The genesis for this book spans both the personal and professional sides of my life. As a psychologist, I spend much
of my time at the hospital bedside caring for children with
cancer, heart disease, and other severe illnesses. Children
suffering from pain teach me profound lessons every day.
They remind me that pain is much more than a neurologi-
cal message traveling from a wound to the brain. Pain, experienced by a child or an adult, is felt in the heart and soul
as well as in the mind. A child's pain is a powerful, often
mystifying experience for the empathic caregiver: one feels
the ache in a child's tummy, yet one can scarcely know what
the child feels. Children's tears compel us to give comfort
and love. Yet what good are hugs and kisses against stomach acid, scraped knees, or shooting migraines?

As a father of three young children, I am challenged to handle physical and emotional bumps and bruises many times each day. I feel it is my responsibility to avoid over- or underreacting to a particular crisis. Instead, I do my best to show compassion and give comfort without overdramatizing the sense of fear and danger evoked at the moment. And yet, I must confess that when my children hurt, I am humbled by my inability to protect them from harm. My son and two daughters each have their own ways of expressing hurt, as well as their shock and disappointment at my having failed to prevent it.

As a young man I found it so difficult to observe severe pain in others that on a few occasions during social hospital visits, I actually passed out! Having harnessed some of that runaway empathy, I have been fortunate to put it to good use. When children (or adults) learn that I am there to be with them *and* their pain, that I believe their pain is real, that I am not afraid of it, that I feel some of it along with them, and that I am there to bring comfort, they give me permission to ease and even help remove their pain.

The questions raised in this book about children's pain are both challenging and rewarding to grapple with. It is my hope that the reader will come away with a better understanding not only of pain, but also of more general issues related to good parenting.

These challenges attracted me to the subject. But understanding children's pain presents us with much more than an intellectual challenge. Untreated and undertreated infant and childhood pain exist in epidemic proportions here in the United States and around the world. Pain can be treated more effectively not only with drugs, but also with human compassion. Heightened awareness of this fact could bring relief and improved quality of life to children and their parents everywhere.

This book is designed to give you, the reader, some tools for understanding and giving care and comfort to a child in pain. These tools will help you and your pediatrician treat routine and emergent pain events with sensitivity, intelligence, and respect for the child's dignity. It will enable many of you to talk with your child about pain, to dispel misconceptions, and to help him or her master fears. Finally, I hope it will stimulate readers to create innovative ways of alleviating pain and to share those innovations with others in your community. While an understanding of pain is in no way the most important part of being a good parent, the emotional tools you use to detect pain and give comfort to your child are indispensable.

How to Use This Book

This book is a guide to help enhance parents' and caregivers' sensitivity to children in pain. Suggestions and ideas are provided to help you better understand why your child experiences pain and how to help alleviate pain when it arises. Because pain is, by definition, a sign that something is wrong in the child's body, it should always be taken seriously. *This book is not intended as a substitute for your child's pediatrician.* Instead, it should be used as a springboard for asking your child, your pediatrician, and yourself questions about pain and how to manage it.

Section I provides a historical overview of the origins of our attitudes toward children's pain, while Section II guides the reader toward a better understanding of what pain is and how it relates to the human body.

Section III illustrates specific instances in which children are confronted with pain in the form of vignettes chosen from the author's experiences. These vignettes present some of the challenges faced by parents and show how a good understanding of common painful situations can help enhance your role as a parent. This third section is organized so that you may identify a life event (like teething or colic) and read through the relevant text for ideas and guidance on how to understand pain issues around that specific event.

Section IV discusses ways of alleviating your child's pain, as well as helping your child prepare for and recover from painful or frightening events, such as getting a flu shot. Parents or caregivers with children who have severe, chronic, or difficult-to-treat health conditions are encouraged to read selections from the bibliography. The reader should feel free to skip to sections relevant to his or her own children.

Section I

Background Information

1

Questions Often Asked About Pain in Children

- What does a mother or father need to observe to know whether a child is in pain? How can a parent determine how severe the pain is?

- Why is it that a newborn breaks into a smile moments after a grueling delivery, or a week-old baby boy sucks peacefully at the breast a few seconds after circumcision?

- Does my newborn baby already feel pain? If the baby feels pain during childbirth, hunger, and teething, will he or she suffer permanent harm from the pain?

- Is circumcision excessively or unnecessarily painful?

- How does a parent's kiss take the pain away from a scraped knee at the playground?

- Why do some children cry out at the slightest provocation, while others tolerate more serious pain without complaint?

- When are the ministrations of parents and caregivers helpful in alleviating pain?

- How can we teach children to understand and become less fearful of the minor and major injuries they experience from day to day?

- How can we teach our children to be better communicators about bodily symptoms of any kind without making them overly concerned?

- Should we encourage boys or girls to refrain from crying when in pain?

- When should children take medication to treat pain?

- How much is too much attention to a child's complaints?

- Under what circumstances should a child be kept home from school when he or she has complained of head or stomach pain?

- Is it ever appropriate to push a child in preparation for competitive sports or musical performance when he or she complains of pain or discomfort associated with rigorous practice?

- What can parents, pediatricians, and dentists do to prepare children for routine immunizations, dental fillings, orthodontia, or any other invasive medical procedures?

- When is pain a sign that something is seriously wrong?

- How much pain is a child expected to tolerate in the case of a broken bone or a sprained joint, or following elective or emergency surgery?

- Can we really ever know what our child goes through when he or she feels pain?

These are a few of the questions that parents and caregivers ask their own parents, each other, and pediatricians when they are faced with a crying child. Everyone comes to his or her own course of action after considering the collective wisdom of the family, the pediatrician's advice, and, most important, experience with that specific child.

No two caregivers react identically to any situation. Often they are both exactly right in their very different responses to a child's pain. Yet, there are many instances where our children come to us with strange complaints, when our usual methods of alleviating pain seem to fail, or when we have difficulty understanding how a doctor diagnosed and treated a child's problem. Pain presents parents and caregivers with thorny challenges. This book summarizes and integrates what is known about children and pain, and how to treat them. I hope to present the information in such a way as to make the reader—whether a parent, nanny, doctor, nurse, or dentist—an intelligent advocate for the care of acute or chronic conditions affecting children in everyday life.

The Power of Comfort

From the moment you bring your baby into the world, you are acutely aware of the fragility of his or her tiny body. For the day or two you spend in the hospital, especially if it is your first baby, it is easy to feel reassured by the presence of doctors, nurses, and high-tech equipment. Even so, the baby's first utterance is usually a big cry or gasping for first breaths. Within minutes after birth, the baby might be given drops in his or her eyes and have blood drawn from his or her heel, bringing vigorous crying from the baby's tiny lungs. As new parents, you might become justifiably concerned that your new baby, only hours old, is already being subjected to painful experiences. Your awareness of the baby's fragility is followed immediately by an enormous feeling of responsibility. If you, the baby's mother and father, cannot protect him or her from these intrusions, then who will?

A Mother's Nurturing

As the child's mother, you quickly learn that there *are* things you can do for your newborn. You may not always be able to protect the baby from painful experiences, but you can provide comfort to help him or her recover from painful moments. You soon learn that every time you pick up your baby and carry her, sway back and forth, stroke her with your hands, sing and coo, or help her suck, you are providing comfort and pleasure.

Soon after you bring the baby home from the hospital, you begin to gain confidence in your power to comfort your baby, to give her pleasure, and to alleviate or mask her pain. After a few days of responding to every cry during the night, you begin to believe that you have a special knack for walking and swaying just the right way to calm and soothe your baby. When Grandmother, very experienced and very eager to help, offers to give you a break and hold the baby after a 3:00 A.M. feeding, you feel suspicious and reluctant to cede responsibility to her. This is because you have begun to get used to your baby's idiosyncrasies and her likes and dislikes.

Likewise, the baby has gotten used to your ways. You know intuitively that Grandmother (unless she has unusual sensitivity) is unlikely to have the same ability to comfort the baby as you do. She may have raised many children in her day, but if she seems not to have the magic touch with your baby right away, it does not necessarily mean she has "lost it." Don't forget that she brought you, too, home from the hospital, and you and she had to become mutually acquainted in the same ways.

Nature made both you and your baby mutually sensitive and adjustable to each other's intimate needs. You have an inborn ability to adapt to each other's rhythms. You might say that your baby "knows" when your breasts are engorged, and that you "know" when your baby is hungry, without having to look or ask. This is a phenomenon called *symbiosis*. It is nature's way of keeping mother and baby attuned to each other. Thinking of it this way, it is easy to see that you are "made" to be sensitive to your child's discomfort. Your ears are tuned in to the special frequency of your child's cry. Your baby's nose is equally tuned in to the scent of your body.

A Father's Sympathetic Pain

Mother Nature, in her mysterious wisdom, guarantees that by the end of the first year of life, many of those mutual sensitivities to smells, rhythms, and sensations gradually diminish and are replaced by modes of communication that are more familiar to adults: language, facial expression, and tone of voice. As the baby develops into toddlerhood, your ability to protect him or her from painful events shrinks day by day.

Watch as a first-time father, bending from the waist, hovers over his 13-month-old who is taking his first steps across the living room floor. Talk about ambivalence! This father is thrilled and terrified at the same time. On the one hand, he is proud that his son is taking off on his own, but on the other, he has never seen the baby use "landing gear." "Now that he has let go of the coffee table," the father wonders, "how will he stop?" So Dad walks bent over, arms outstretched, in hopes of catching the boy and breaking his fall.

He holds his breath every time it looks as if the boy is about to take a spill, and worries that a bump or a bruise could harm the spirit of his fragile-looking toddler, causing him to give up on his intrepid efforts to walk. "If only I can protect him long enough," reasons the father to himself, "he'll gain confidence and then I can relax."

Within five minutes, the father has a sore back, but the baby continues to experiment. The father no longer follows with his body, but now keeps vigil with his eyes. For days, every time his child drops down on his behind, the father gasps. He soon learns that by allowing his son to risk hurting himself (within reasonable limits of safety), the child will gain independence and self-reliance. He will grow physically and emotionally. And, very important, he will develop an ability to tolerate painful experiences as they arise.

Amazingly, even after days and weeks of bumps and bruises as the toddler learns to crawl and walk, he continues to believe with perfect faith that his parent can protect him from harm. When he actually does fall hard and bumps his nose against the coffee table, he appears stunned by the very possibility that such a thing could happen to him. Or, perhaps it is you, his father, who thinks: "How could I let this happen? I must be a failure as father and protector if I let my little boy get a bloody nose."

This is a prototypical event in your development as a parent. It is at that moment you realize that there is only so much you can do to *prevent* your child from experiencing pain. But then you pick him up, say soothing words, hold him close, doctor his nose, and say words to convince yourself that all will be OK. Now you are reminded that your power to comfort is still great. Only, now the source of your power lies more in your ability to relate to your child in a caring way, even during a little crisis.

Understanding and Talking About Pain with Children: Emily's Limp

A good understanding of the way pain works and what it means to you and your child can be useful. Imagine yourself the mother of 10-year-old Emily. Emily is enthusiastic about her upcoming ballet performance. She practices diligently every day, perhaps a bit too diligently. You drive to her ballet school to pick her up, and she walks gingerly, almost limping, to the car. Though she tries to hide any sign of discomfort in her face, you sense that this girl is in significant pain. Do you say something? Do you express your concern? Do you forbid her to perform when injured? Do you praise her for her courage and persistence? Why does she try to hide her pain from you? Is she afraid you will not let her perform, or that you will think she is exaggerating to avoid performing? How can you find out the exact nature of her pain?

As her mother, you have a responsibility to guide and protect Emily from making poor judgments about her health and well-being. Her limp could be a result of routine soreness and fatigue, or it could be an indication of an athletic injury which, if ignored, could cause more serious damage. The way you respond to Emily's limp must take into account her need for independence as well. If you decide to comment on it, she could reject your concern and insist that she'll be OK. Nevertheless, you may well interpret Emily's limp as a silent request to skip her performance, that her teachers are pushing her too hard. If you express your concern in a way that conveys your understanding of what is contributing to the pain in her leg, your daughter is likely to feel more understood and be more receptive to your help.

What goes into a thoughtful approach to a child with painful symptoms? Pretty much the same thing that goes into good communication in general. As you will see in each section of this book, a good way to start is by watching and listening. In Emily's case, for example, you might ask how she is feeling instead of telling her how you think her leg must feel. You might say that you noticed the way she was walking and wondered about it. You then would want to give her a chance to describe how her leg feels. If she is in pain, how does she feel about that? Ideally, you can help Emily come to a well-reasoned decision about how to alleviate the pain herself. If, on the other hand, you feel that she could endanger herself by continuing to dance, you could make the decision for her or seek the advice of her coach or a physician.

2

Centuries of Neglect/ Recent Developments

Your beliefs about children's pain are rooted in your upbringing as well as your inborn instincts. Until very recently, children were treated by society and by medical science as miniature adults. If your parents or grandparents grew up before the 1930s, they may have begun working at ages as young as eight years old in unsanitary conditions and for long hours, receiving very little pay in sweatshops, mines, and factories, and on farms. If they suffered physical injury or disease on the job, they had to fend for themselves. Care and compassion was available from some individuals, families, and charities; however, it was not the norm.

The way you treat your child when he or she is in pain or needs nurturing from you reflects the way your parents raised you, the way your grandparents raised them, and so on. Left to your own natural devices, you will act in accordance with your parents' and grandparents' beliefs when a crying child calls for your attention.

For instance, you might insist that the child stop crying immediately so you can treat a bleeding cut, or you might become angry at your child because you think he or she "should" be able to tolerate the pain better. If you become frustrated by your child's incessant crying, you might want to "snap him out of it" with a shake or (perish the thought) a slap. You might choose to punish the child for dangerous behavior that led to a painful mishap, shifting the focus of attention away from the pain. On the other hand, if you operate under the assumption that the pain resides in the bruise or the cut itself, you might treat the injury without attending to the child's emotional response to it.

Historical Events and Social Reforms

Public education for the masses emerged in western Europe as recently as the early nineteenth century. Before that era, society did not attend to the health and welfare of children as a group.

During the 1800s, when children started to emerge from the shadows of substandard living conditions to attend school, communities began to place greater importance on children's health and welfare. Agencies were founded to advocate for child welfare in the late nineteenth and early twentieth centuries, and social reforms such as Roosevelt's New Deal and Lyndon Johnson's Great Society changed the way we value our young. Today, programs such as Head Start and the Adoption Assistance and Child Welfare Act of 1980 continue to shine the spotlight on children's health issues.

Reforms during the early 1970s and '80s have made it possible to prosecute perpetrators of physical and sexual abuse within families. Now that child abuse and child welfare are in the public eye, we have begun, for the first time, to face the challenge of healing severe pain inflicted on children. After centuries of neglect, we now believe that all children deserve to have their basic physical and emotional needs met so they can enjoy a safe, nurturing childhood in preparation for a productive role in society.

Advances in Medicine: A Mixed Blessing

Thanks to advances in modern medicine, more children can expect better pain relief and pain management than ever before. As these children grow to adulthood, they will no doubt come to expect the same for their children and for future generations.

As previously mentioned, before the advent of modern medicine, physicians followed society's lead in treating children as though they were miniature adults. Children in your grandparents' time died at early ages of a myriad of diseases. Before there were vaccines and antibiotics, generations were wiped out by epidemics of flu, smallpox, measles, rubella, and polio, to mention only a few scourges. It is likely that your great grandparents conceived many children in the hope that a few would be carried to term, survive to adulthood, and support them in old age.

Yet while the death of a child was certainly as painful a loss a hundred years ago as it is today, society tended to minimize the value of children. Children were treated as replaceable commodities, considered sources of cheap labor, and disciplined like domestic animals. Ideal character traits in our society were toughness, resiliency, individualism, and resourcefulness. Vulnerability and dependency on others were signs of weakness: tolerated in women and children; abhorred in adult men.

Your grandparents' family doctor was surgeon, internist, obstetrician, and pediatrician, all rolled into one. He was also a man, replete with male biases, about boys not crying and girls being histrionic. Even after the advent of general anesthesia, surgery was performed on children quickly to prevent undue pain, but without sedation. Until as recently as 1960, surgeons rationalized that children neither feel nor remember painful experiences the way adults do.

To this day, pediatricians often rely on medications approved for adults to treat many childhood ailments, including severe pain. Because many of these medications are as yet untested on children, pediatricians must make educated guesses when writing prescriptions. One unfortunate result of this is a general tendency to undertreat children's pain.

Now, your parents and grandparents might argue that they survived, and they would be correct, but only up to a point. The idea that "suffering is good for us" stems from deep-rooted cultural and religious beliefs. The problem is, we may be confusing moral suffering with physical pain. There is evidence that physical and mental suffering take a toll on the growth and development of children. Recent scientific inquiry has revealed the benefit of sparing babies and children from unnecessary pain.

A good illustration of this point is the tonsillectomy. Before 1965, most children in the United States had their tonsils removed, before the age of five or six, as a precaution against infections in the throat. Even after surgery under general anesthesia had become standard practice, the principal pain reliever for the postoperative sore throat was vanilla ice cream. Children were kept in the hospital for several days in case of hemorrhage or infection and then released.

We now know that injuries, inflicted either surgically or by accident, cause temporary impairment of the body's ability to heal itself. Untreated pain further compromises the healing process. It should not be a surprise, then, that more aggressive control of postoperative pain actually *speeds healing* and *reduces the likelihood of infections* at the surgical site. If this is true for postoperative recovery, perhaps it is also true when your child falls and bumps his or her head on the floor. Less pain means less fear, less distress, and less suffering for all involved.

The last half-century has witnessed an unprecedented drop in the infant mortality rate. Children born during the baby boom and afterward were the first to have a pediatrician as a doctor. They also had access to specialists in pediatric surgery, radiology, cardiology, oncology, neurology, orthopedics, pulmonology, and endocrinology, to mention only a few.

Some of the benefits your children reap from the past quarter-century's advances in medicine include the use of general anesthesia for children undergoing surgery, better drugs to control pain, and lower risk of medical complications due to poorly controlled pain.

The past quarter-century has also seen dramatic improvements in cure rates for once-fatal conditions such as childhood leukemia. Children can receive a transplanted heart, lung, liver, kidney, pancreas, or bone marrow with promise of significant but as yet undetermined extension of life. These dramatic and wonderful advances have come, however, at some cost.

The Downside of Modern Medicine

Doctors may not have known how to cure diseases or how to alleviate pain before the modern medical revolution, but they did know how to care for the sick. Your grandfather's doctor knew that even if a disease could not be cured, your young grandfather still needed comfort, care, human touch, hope, and, above all, a sense that the world around him remained normal in the face of crisis.

The family doctor visited your grandfather in his own home. He examined him with his own senses: sight, touch, hearing, and smell. Observed in this way, the symptoms took on an immediacy that is lost in the world of modern technology. The doctor made a diagnosis, and failing a cure, turned the caregiving over to your grandfather's mom and dad. Unless surgery was indicated, there was little the doctor could do that the family could not also do under his guidance. A child's personal experience of illness was heavily influenced by the way his loved ones cared for him, and not by the length of stay in a distant hospital.

Although disease could not be cured and pain was given short shrift, *suffering* was better understood a century ago than it is today. Suffering occurs when there is pain without comfort or without hope. Your grandfather may have felt pain when he was in bed with pneumonia as a young boy. Even if there were no adequate painkillers, *his* mother and father had the wherewithal to alleviate his suffering with love and compassion. When modern medicine introduced technological advances, doctors no longer needed to touch their patients as much. They began to rely more heavily on laboratory findings than on clinical intuition for making a diagnosis. As a profession, doctors forgot some of their people skills and yet were slow to embrace newfound methods of reducing children's pain. Today, if your own child lies in bed with a broken leg, he or she may suffer, even with adequate pain relief, if there is not sufficient emotional support.

As a parent or caregiver, you have the opportunity to offer your children the benefits of modern medicine combined with good, old-fashioned TLC.

Facing Up to Pain

Even with advances in modern science, the attitudes of many physicians and parents have not completely caught up. Some still carry the belief that babies do not feel pain or, if they do, do not remember painful experiences. In spite of hundreds of new pain-relief products available on the market, there is still an obstacle to controlling pain: our own beliefs. How can a just and humane society rationalize neglect of children's pain and suffering when it possesses tools to alleviate both?

Perhaps the idea of pain threatens our inner sense of well-being. Pain means that something is going awry in the body. If your child hurts, you take it as evidence of trouble somewhere. Until pain surfaces into conscious awareness, however, it is convenient to imagine that we are invulnerable. It is relatively easy to go through our days oblivious to the fact that our bodies and our children's bodies can suffer harm. Ernest Becker, in his book *Denial of Death*, describes this unawareness as an emotional defense against the inevitable; against mortality. Every physical insult to the body—every injury, every illness—and the scars and antibodies they leave behind are markers on the journey from the unspoiled innocence of infancy to the decline of old age. We feel the weight of extra responsibility for the welfare of our children because they have not yet learned to fear their mortality.

Pain is also a threat to our belief that all problems have a solution. Sherwin Nuland sheds light on this subject in his book *How We Die*. On the one hand, modern society has embraced perpetual youth and swept death under the carpet. Science and technology foster the illusion that there is a rational explanation for everything and a solution to every problem. The fact that humans are plagued with incurable illnesses, as well as untreatable symptoms of some of those illnesses, creates problems for an overly rational, scientific way of thinking. Physicians are trained to diagnose and cure disorders of the human body. Many are at a loss, however, when there is nothing left to be done for a child except wait for a virus to run its course. At times like this, the physician leaves us to care for pain and suffering.

On the other hand, the media capitalize on society's fascination with the afterlife, reincarnation, the supernatural, and accounts of those who have "cheated" death. This obsession is just the flip side of our difficulty in facing the fact that as our children grow, we have less and less control over their safety and well-being. We like to think that children are guaranteed a long life ahead. "Perish the thought," we say when we hear of a calamity befalling someone else's child. "There but for the grace of God go I." Cultures worldwide have expressions conveying this denial that one's own family and loved ones can be vulnerable to danger.

Pain is both a *signal* and a *symbol*. It is a signal that something is wrong somewhere in the body, and it alerts the body to go into action to avoid immediate danger that might be causing damage. If we heed the alert, we often face the limits of our ability escape harm.

Pain is also a symbol of that weakness and vulnerability. It is our Achilles' heel reminding us of our mortality. We deny the presence of pain. We deny its severity. We deny its very meaning. To care adequately for pain, our own or that of our children, we must be willing to face up to its meaning. It is a strange paradox. Opening ourselves up to our human vulnerability allows us to be more compassionate toward others. By analogy, it is important to get beyond the fear of the sight of blood if one is required to bandage a wound!

The fact is that *children feel pain*. Children remember pain. Untreated pain, whether acute or chronic, physical, emotional, or spiritual, can take a significant toll on a child's body and soul. Children's suffering requires the same care and compassion as adult suffering. An important first step toward a better understanding of your own children's health care is to realize that management of pain is not a luxury or hedonistic, but rather a basic need shared by all.

Toward a Holistic Perspective

The growing popularity of holistic approaches to health has helped reacquaint us with the fact that pain is an essential part of life; that by facing pain's signal and symbolic meanings, we can learn how to better alleviate suffering. Family practitioners, pediatricians, pediatric dentists, and psychologists specializing in pediatric medicine have begun to take children's pain more seriously. Two seminal texts have been written in the last decade on children's pain: *Pain in Children: Nature, Assessment, and Treatment* by Patricia A. McGrath and *Childhood Pain: Current Issues, Research, and Management* by D. M. Ross and S. A. Ross. New journals, including the *Journal of Pain and Symptom Management* and *Pediatric Psychology*, have devoted entire issues to the subject.

This trend represents a welcome return to the "art of healing" as it intertwines itself with the technology of curing. Classical approaches to pain have been atomistic and compartmentalized. Scientific methods lead us to break the puzzle of pain down to its smallest parts: pain receptors, sensory pathways, neurotransmitters, and brain centers.

While this aspect of scientific development is absolutely essential, it causes us to forget that we are much more than the sum of our parts.

Therapists who specialize in pain management know that a good explanation of how pain works must incorporate concepts like experience, learning, consciousness, awareness, and meaning. These concepts are hard to define and even harder to study scientifically. Yet that is just what pain practitioners and researchers do as they evaluate factors that increase pain and suffering, as well as factors that provide relief.

Until recently, Western science has scoffed at practitioners of healing arts and traditions from other parts of the world, i.e., the healing arts of traditional cultures developed over centuries. They are not the product of modern scientific inquiry, but have developed from the cumulative wisdom of shamans, midwives, and folk-healers. Now that medical scientists have begun to test some traditional healing methods for safety and efficacy, we find that ancient traditions have a great deal to offer. A problem arises when people have no way to make an educated choice among the dozens of health and healing traditions that fall outside the realm of modern medicine. I will review some holistic options available for children in Chapter 17.

Section II

*W*hat Is Pain?

3

A Working Definition
of Pain

The way you treat your boy or girl when he or she complains of a tummyache or headache depends in large measure on what you think pain is, what causes it, and what kind of pain merits what kinds of complaints. It is helpful to think about your own definition of pain, compare it with that of your child, and finally with the definition in this chapter.

Pain comes from the Latin word *poena* (as in penalty), meaning punishment. I find this rather amusing, since young children tend to assume the reason for an ache or a pain is parental or devine retribution for some wrongdoing. Dictionary definitions tell us little of what physical pain is, where it comes from, or how it feels. Physical and mental aspects of pain are difficult to distinguish. This is a true reflection of pain's place in the borderland between the physical and the mental, between stimulus and response, between cause and effect.

Let us turn to a more comprehensive definition of pain. We might want to call this a "working definition" because there is still a great deal to be learned about what exactly pain is, how we feel it, what makes it feel worse or better, and how we alleviate it. A good definition should be specific enough to be useful, but broad enough to encompass the true complexity of pain experience. The following definition is based on a *biopsychosocial* model of pain. That means that in defining pain, we take three general factors into account: the body, the mind, and society (i.e., other people).

The International Association for the Study of Pain defines pain as "(an) unpleasant sensory and emotional experience associated with actual or potential tissue damage or described in terms of such damage." This definition incorporates the emotional and physical components of pain in its objective and subjective aspects.

Breaking down the definition piece-by-piece illustrates some of the aspects of pain to think about when your child hurts.

Unpleasant: You know your child is experiencing something unpleasant by his or her emotional expression, language, and behavior. There are many unpleasant sensations that are not painful; e.g., when your child sticks his hand into someone's leftover chewing gum in the movie theater, he grimaces from disgust, not pain! If he catches his finger in a doorway and grimaces the same way, you infer from the context of your own experience that it signifies pain.

Sensory: Your child's pain is a physical *feeling*. This type of feeling usually gets into your child's body through the nervous system, through her *sense* of touch, and through her body's ability to detect harm or damage somewhere on its surface or inside. As with unpleasantness, sensations are purely subjective. The difference is that biologists can trace specific nerve pathways that carry sensory information from the sensory organs (eyes, ears, and skin) to various centers in the brain.

Emotional experience: In addition to being a physical sensation, pain is an inherently negative emotional experience. We humans are naturally designed to seek pleasure and avoid pain. One way nature ensured that we would avoid pain is to associate painful sensation with bad feelings. We remember feelings better than sensations. In fact, we rely on our emotional interest to remember just about anything from new words to new faces. In understanding children's pain, it is helpful to know that children do not have the same clear distinction between physical and emotional aspects of pain as do adults. Your child might "feel" pain from a sore stomach in his "heart" as well. He may tell you that something you said to him hurts, and really mean that he feels pain.

Associated with actual or potential tissue damage: Your baby's gums are inflamed from teething and send a pain message to the brain every time she bites on the nipple. Here, actual tissue damage causes your baby to feel pain. Pain sensations often persist well after the inflammation is gone. That is why the same baby might resist biting down on the nipple the next day. It is as if she "knows" that stimulating inflamed gums could cause more damage.

Her feeling of pain also leads her to treat the tissue more carefully once it has healed. Pain from *potential* tissue damage can feel just like pain from *actual* tissue damage. In both cases, the same "pain centers" in the brain are activated, and the same memory trace of past pain is awakened.

Inclusion of the word *potential* in the definition helps explain the protective function of pain. A boy who has sprained his ankle playing basketball knows that his ankle will hurt if he puts weight on it. His posture, his choice of activities, his feelings, and his emotions are all heavily affected by *potential* pain. He may not feel pain now, but his ankle will hurt every time he puts weight on it.

Or described in terms of such damage: Sometimes children feel pain in the absence of any known tissue damage. Your five-year-old boy might say, for example: "I hurt so bad, I feel like my heart is burning up." To really understand children's pain, it is absolutely necessary to put "metaphorical" pain in the same category as actual physical pain. The boy in this example hurts just as much as if there were a real fire there.

In another instance, a girl might wake up after sleeping on top of her arm. As the blood begins to rush back in, she says: "It hurts like somebody stuck pins and needles all over my hand and arm." We know that nobody stuck pins into her, but her description is useful and accurate in assessing what kind of pain she feels.

Before modern medicine, pain was understood very differently from the way it is today. People interpreted pain and disease as something alien invading the body or soul. That something was not an airborne virus, but a bad spirit. The spirit could have intent, purpose, even personality. In this way, it was easy to think of illness as a punishment for wrongdoing, or even an arbitrary act of an angry god. This type of thinking is called *animism*, which means giving human or spiritual characteristics to physical processes. According to animistic thinking, pain is not a feeling felt by an individual. Rather, it is an alien spirit invading that individual.

Young children are little animists. They may feel pain not only as a simple sensation, but as a punishment by a bad being in the afflicted area. "Get it out of my belly; I'll be good," a three-year-old might say. When your five-year-old says, "Daddy, I feel bad in the head," she might have pain, but she might *mean* that there is something evil going on in her. As a parent, you might be amused by this. But until little more than a century ago, adults were just as likely to interpret pain in this way. Even well-educated modern parents may not be entirely rid of the archaic belief in possession by spirits.

One way to examine your own beliefs as a parent is to ask yourself how you feel when your child is complaining of pain. Do you feel that there is a purely biophysical problem that the pain indicates a need to solve? Or, to what extent do you feel that the situation is "bad"; that there is a shadow cast over your child's being that must be lifted with the pain? Do you want to blame the pain on the child's babysitter taking poor care of the child, and does the blame and recrimination overshadow the symptoms themselves? Perhaps there is some deeper truth to the idea of pain and illness being more than just physiology after all.

To adequately define pain is to understand the connection between body and mind. That is the problem of how, when he accidentally bites his tongue, your four-year-old becomes aware of and verbalizes that his tongue has been damaged. He can express that it is bothering him and causing distress, and that something must be done about it *now*. The mind/body connection also explains how the same four-year-old's memory of biting his tongue can reactivate his fear and pain hours later.

Ask a child what pain is and you will get some very interesting answers. Although we cannot ask a preverbal infant, we can guess that to him, pain is a combination of fear, foreboding, malaise, and the particular bodily sensation associated with those feelings. When a 10-month-old infant feels hunger pangs, we cannot be sure that he actually locates the stomach as the source of his pain. To a baby, the body is not yet a clearly physical object with volume, occupying space in the room. The stomach is vaguely part of the baby's whole world, just as his image of Mommy is part of his whole world.

To a three-year-old with a scraped knee, the pain is the scrape, the blood, the sensation, Mommy picking him up, and the bandage she put on the cut, all wrapped up into one jumbled feeling. Unlike an adult, a three-year-old's concept of the body does not include the concept of pain as a temporary episode of discomfort from a local irritation. To the child, this distressing moment might just as well be the beginning of an eternity of pain. What, after all, is the difference between a minute and a day for a three-year-old?

Physicians are mainly concerned with discovering why many patients who have the *same* ailment have the *same* kind of pain and discomfort. In this way, doctors discover how to diagnose problems based on typical symptoms and treat them according to a set of rules and decisions. Thus, ear pain suggests your child might have an ear infection. Joint pain suggests a rheumatic condition. Treatments for these problems correctly aim at the cause of the problem rather than the symptoms. Painkillers alone would be an irresponsible treatment for an ear infection. However, physicians tend to work under the assumption that the mind is really nothing but a part of the body and is a product of the brain's functioning. This implies that there is nothing that happens in the mind that cannot be explained by physical processes in the brain and body.

Psychologists, in contrast to physicians, are intrigued with the fact that two children with the same physical problem may experience different levels of pain. Medical science pursues the reason why two different children feel the type of pain they do, but cannot explain why a patient experiences hearing loss due to a severe but otherwise asymptomatic ear infection. The problem is that modern medicine has been reluctant to include the mind in its understanding of pain.

Until a hundred years ago, no one knew how information got from one place to another in your child's body. Most thought that when someone stepped on your foot, a shock was sent through muscles or tendons to the knee, causing it to bend up reflexively, and to the vocal chords for their reflexive yell: "Ouch!" As scientists began to understand the importance of the brain, they discovered that the brain and the nerves in the toes are two opposite ends of the same busy street. The brain processes several messages at once: that something painful just happened on a particular spot on the body, that a reflex did or did not go into effect, and that the pain is a new or familiar experience.

Now we have established a working definition of pain: "(an) unpleasant sensory and emotional experience associated with actual or potential tissue damage or described in terms of such damage." This definition will help us keep in mind the roles of feelings, emotions, and the brain as they all relate to your child's experience of pain and pain relief.

4

Why We Need Pain

The Helpless Infant

Our ability to feel pain is life-sustaining. From the moment of birth, we are bombarded with an overwhelming variety of sensations: some painful, some pleasurable. Without pain to protect us we would live in constant danger. Our automatic reflexes comprise the more primitive components of our nervous system. This means that we share these self-protective abilities with a few plants and nearly all animals. Reflexes already function in the unborn fetus when it reacts to light, sound, and physical stimulation within the mother's uterus. While it is true that we are born with a fairly well-developed ability to protect our body from immediate dangers, we have a great deal to learn from life experience.

It is easier to understand the value of pain as adults. When we feel pain, we respond reflexively by avoiding its source. Then we identify its cause, if possible, and take further measures to protect ourselves. Infants have the same sensations and reflexes, but, without learning life's hard lessons, they don't have the capacity to evaluate, identify, and take measures to avoid further danger. An infant's body automatically recoils at a loud noise, a sudden bump, or a poke. A baby's hand pulls away from heat. His eyes shut at excessive light or wind. A baby dropped into water reacts reflexively to protect himself against suffocation and cold. Heartbeat and respiration slow down, allowing precious seconds and even minutes for lifesaving rescue. Even without adults around for protection, these built-in safety mechanisms afford new babies a measure of protection from the elements.

Babies have the same sensations of pain as adults but lack the ability to avoid its source or to understand it. This is one reason why babies are lost without the nurturing care, feeding, warmth, and physical contact instinctively provided by their parents. The cries of a healthy baby who is wet or hungry could curdle the blood of all but the most insensitive adult.

The mere thought of her child's cry is sufficient to stimulate a lactating mother's "let-down" reflex. For example, a friend of mine was riding home from work on the New York City subway, happily daydreaming about her infant waiting at home, until the passenger seated next to her noticed a thin whitish liquid trickling down her newspaper into her lap. Awakened from her reverie with a bewildered "excuse me" from the other passenger, my friend realized that her thoughts had led to an overflow of breast milk. If the *thought* of a baby's hunger is sufficient to activate the flow of mother's milk, imagine how powerful the sound of a baby's cry is to stir parents into protective action! Mothers of newborns trade stories of husbands who sleep through their baby's cries while they, the mothers, seem to wake up seconds before or at the very moment of the baby's first whimper in the middle of the night.

These stories are wondrous, but not mysterious. The usefulness of a child's cry is obvious. It expresses his or her immediate feelings and brings assistance from caregivers in the form of warmth, nutrition, body contact, hygiene, and safety from external danger. Parents are often able to pick out the signal of their child's cry from the background noise of equally loud cries of other children. The natural art of parenting has evolved to ensure that good nurturers have a genetically competitive advantage. Parents who are better able to care for their young have a better chance of perpetuating their own family stock through those children. A parent, therefore, who is attuned to the health and comfort of his or her children and who responds appropriately to pain signals is at a competitive advantage over other parents.

Likewise, babies and children whose cries and movements are most effective at bringing food and safety from adults are more likely to grow to adulthood themselves and have their own babies. Babies and children who, when they get hurt or sick and feel pain, are best able to communicate that to their caregivers will likewise "select" themselves for passing on successful genes to the next generation of babies and children.

Mothers know that breast-feeding provides almost immediate comfort to a distressed baby. Some scientists now believe that in addition to providing essential nutrients, breast milk may contain natural painkillers. Some have observed a topical analgesic effect on gum pain from teething, and most mothers confirm what appears to be an overall euphoric and sedating effect on very distressed babies. This observation has led to research on the presence of intrinsic opiates (called endorphins) in breast milk. Conversely, babies who receive insufficient physical contact with caregivers are vulnerable to sickness, slowed growth, and even death.

Vignette: Baby Carlos's Cry Initiates Ella into Motherhood

Ella, age 24, a new mother, lives in a North American city, far away from her family and friends. Her husband, Juan, is reluctantly out of town on urgent business. It is two in the morning. Three-week-old Carlos whimpers half-sleeping in the bed next to Ella.

He had cried loudly for an hour and a half between midnight and 1:30 A.M., and nothing seemed to console him. Many thoughts and fears, both logical and emotional, raced through Ella's mind while he wailed: Was he wet? No. Hungry? Perhaps, but too distraught to eat. If he was hungry, did the pangs hurt? If so, was Carlos afraid? If he was afraid, did I somehow let him down?

At 1:30, Carlos stopped crying. Did the discomfort go away? Or did little Carlos merely exhaust himself back to sleep? What will he be like when he wakes up in a half hour for his next feeding? Will he still be distressed? Will I be up to the task of comforting him?

Ella's heart begins to pound. Is he sick? Should I ring the doctor? Will he wake up at all? Soon Ella is crying. She is alone, inexperienced, and vulnerable to the hormonal imbalances that accompany the postpartum period following birth. In a near panic, Ella calls her mother, waking her in Venezuela. In a few minutes, Carlos is awake, feeding contentedly at Ella's breast. Ella laughs at herself with her mother still on the line.

Carlos's behavior is much like that of most three-week-olds. Ella's thoughts and feeling are *absolutely normal*. This story illustrates the challenge babies present to us every day. Without language we must rely on our intuition and the advice of our friends and family. Together, we try as best we can to sufficiently nurture our babies.

Crying is a signal. It alerts us to a child's distress. We intuitively know that a crying baby probably means a baby in pain. There are important differences between our own experience of pain and those of infants and small children. When adults feel pain, we understand two things at once: something is wrong and it is localized somewhere on or in the body. In addition, we can distinguish between *types* of pain (hot, aching throbbing, etc.). (These types will be explained in more detail in Chapter 5.) When a child cries out, we as caregivers are placed at a disadvantage. The cry itself does not tell us what hurts or where it hurts. To make matters worse, the child can not always tell us what or where the problem is.

The child's cry grabs the caregiver's attention. The cry leads the parent to visually examine the child and to run down a mental list of possible reasons for the distress. Is the baby (or child) hungry, wet, stuck, frustrated, sore, sick, injured, or annoyed? (A more complete description of how to assess pain appears in Chapter 14.)

Notice that the list includes both emotional and physical sources of pain and distress. Visual examination can rule out some, but not all, of the possible reasons for the cry. If the child is verbal, he or she may be able to give some indication of what the source of the problem is.

Every parent can confirm what a comfort it is when his or her child is finally able to verbalize a problem. I call it the "Age of Relief," usually somewhere during the child's third year. The onset of the Age of Relief roughly coincides with completion of toilet training and is the first indication of the child's ability to localize and describe sensations in parts of the body.

However, in times of crisis even a verbal child may be too confused or upset to be an accurate reporter. The adult's next recourse is to try a few different ways to calm the child. Each parent initiates a routine soon after the baby is born and gradually develops it as the baby grows and becomes more communicative.

The choices are narrower for a newborn. Usually we check the diaper for wetness, the bottom for rash, or try feeding, burping, snuggling, or just moving around. We let the baby's response be the guide to whether we have applied the correct solution and infer backward to the cause of the problem. We sometimes might infer incorrectly, but it does not matter as long as the baby has stopped crying. When a child repeatedly associates a caregiver's ministrations with feelings of warmth, comfort, and safety, he or she identifies the intentional or incidental relief from pain with those good feelings. As many parents know, "mere" expressions of love—gentle caresses and hugs—are potent analgesics.

We need pain to goad us into action when a physical (i.e., medical) problem is not obvious to the naked eye. There are situations in which a child's subjective experience of pain is the only evidence available to detect what could become a serious illness. For example, early stages of meningitis begin with neck and head pain and early appendicitis starts with lower abdominal pain. Even a bone fracture may cause no obvious impairment to a child's activities with the exception of a feeling of pain.

*V*ignette: Billy's Stomach Pain Makes Itself Visible

How does pain lead to healing in children? Billy, 10 years old, wakes up on a school day with a stomachache. He does not look happy to get out of bed. Stomach pain makes him want to lie still. Moving seems to make it worse. His mother notices this as well as the look on his face. He is scowling and grumbling. Because he does not want to miss an important class trip, he does not tell his mother why he is grumbling. Nevertheless, she "feels" that something is wrong. Billy's stomach tells him to skip breakfast. Stomach pain sends a self-protective message to the appetite centers of the brain to delay eating until the problem is taken care of. This makes intuitive sense from a biological and medical point of view. A sick stomach might be inflamed, be poisoned, have a virus, or have an ulcer, none of which are helped by the exertion required to digest more food. In fact, severe pain can cause the stomach to empty itself through vomiting or diarrhea, leaving it empty while it tries to heal itself or be healed by medicine.

Your Child's Nervous System

The late nineteenth and early twentieth centuries saw a revolution in understanding of the nervous system. It is useful to take a brief side trip into the workings of this intricate web of cells and synapses. Technical portions may be skipped without much loss of general understanding. Some readers may, however, wish to explore this area for a better grasp of how the body registers pain.

When your child is in pain, your child's brain "knows" where on or in the body the painful sensation is coming from, as well as roughly what type of pain it is, and how severe. Advances in medicine, anesthesia, and brain surgery have brought intriguing new information. Brain surgeons have observed that patients under local anesthesia can describe sensations over different areas of the body when specific spots on the surface of an area of the exposed brain (called the sensory cortex) are touched by a probe. Probing the area governing motor skills causes specific parts of the body to twitch involuntarily. Injuries in those areas lead to loss of motor control, or, in some cases, total paralysis in the corresponding area of the body. Wounded portions of the sensory cortex lead to an inability to feel sensation (or pain) in the corresponding area on the surface of the body.

A "map" created by neurophysiologists lays out in two dimensions an upside-down, distorted image of the human body across the sensory and motor areas on the surface of the brain. This image has been called the "homunculus," or little human. The distortion of the image shows that more sensitive body areas, such as the fingers and mouth, occupy a relatively large proportion of area on the map, while less sensitive areas on the legs and torso appear relatively truncated. More sensitive areas of the body are specialized to discriminate among subtle differences in sensation and feeling. Those areas understandably occupy more space in the brain.

How Does Sensory Information Get into the Body?

The idea that there is a sensory/motor pattern on the surface of the brain shaped like a funny-looking, inverted person has fueled many people's fantasies that there is indeed a "little human" at the controls telling us when to move, what to feel, and so forth.

The value of discovering the homunculus was in learning how our nervous system sends messages between the brain and the rest of the body, and vice versa. That information, by itself, was not enough. Neurophysiologists further questioned *how* heat that burns a child's finger, sunlight that hurts a baby's eyes, physical energy from a bottle dropped on a toddler's bare foot, or pressure on the child's eardrum get converted into a pain message to the brain.

There is a specialized subgroup of nerve cells that are activated when you are poked, pinched, or punched. These cells convey pain information to the central nervous system (i.e., the brain). There is more than one kind of pain receptor. If you stub your toe, one nerve cell triggers the reflex of pulling back the foot and may not be associated directly with pain per se. Another type gives rise to the first pain sensation you feel, akin to a shock. Perhaps, with experience, one feels this to be a warning of the next sensation triggered by yet a different type of receptor. The third sensation is the aching, throbbing pain that may last for a few minutes after the mishap.

How Does Your Child Become Aware of Pain?

When the tip of your child's finger is pricked by a thorn or a doctor's needle, a nerve ending just beneath the skin is irritated, and nerve cells carry information about that irritation via the spine to the brain. Called *neurons*, these cells are found throughout the human body. Their special function is to carry sensory and pain information from the various parts of the body to the spine, to the brain, and back again.

When stimulated, neurons "switch on," or, in physiologists' terms, *fire*. When a neuron fires, the impulse only needs to reach the spine before it begins to perform its protective duty. Without benefit of the brain, the spine can trigger a reflex. In the case of the thorn in the finger, the reflex is to recoil the arm muscles. If nature works correctly, this will cause the finger to be pulled away from the thorn and any further danger.

The spine and the brain work together to make sure that painful events lead to appropriate avoidance and withdrawal reflexes, that we learn quickly from painful experiences (usually in one try), and that useful information gets to the brain about the quality, intensity, and location of the pain.

The Synapse

How does the nerve impulse travel *between* neurons? Going back to the thorn, the neurons beneath the skin on the fingertip convert the mechanical energy of the pressure from the thorn into the electrochemical energy of the nerve impulse. These receptor cells are quite small and represent only the beginning of the long circuit between the brain and source of pain.

Before the message reaches consciousness that the thorn has injured the finger, it must travel through many nerve cell bodies. Until recently, we did not know how the signal got from the end of one neuron to the beginning of the next. Neurons are bathed in a fluid filled with a large number of chemical substances called *neurotransmitters*. These are the molecules that carry the nerve message between nerve cells.

What do neurotransmitters have to do with pain? Everything. Some neurotransmitters pass information from the toe to the spine and brain about the pain. Others carry pain-killing information from the brain to affected parts of the body.

Now it is possible to understand how the same type of thorn can cause two completely different kinds of pain experience. In 1965, R. Melzack and P. D. Wall accurately guessed that the central nervous system has a way of blocking out some pain sensation from awareness. This blocking had to occur without shutting down the whole system, so the individual could continue to function. This point is illustrated in the following vignette.

Vignette: In the Heat of Battle

Jerry, a rough-and-tumble eight-year-old, was in his glory playing center-forward in a semifinal match of his town's soccer championship. With the score tied and three minutes left to play on the clock, Jerry received a perfect pass and charged the goal. He knew that the opposing goalie, a lanky nine-year-old girl named Anna, would be a daunting obstacle. A brilliant "head fake" brought Jerry around the defenseman. Just as Jerry made his final charge to the goal, Anna ran out to block his kick and the two children collided with a loud thud. Parents and teammates cheered as the ball sailed into the upper corner of the goal. In the tremendous excitement, Jerry had yet to notice several severe bruises he received in the collision, nor did Anna feel the lump rising on her forehead or the sprain in her left wrist. Yes, Jerry and Anna felt pain a short time later, but no one was surprised by the delay. In less exciting circumstances, the same injuries would surely have brought instant, acute pain to both children. Similar stories have often been told of soldiers wounded in the heat of battle who denied the slightest hint of pain until they were evacuated from the field many hours later.

What is going on here? Two converging streams of evidence help to explain how awareness of pain can be temporarily abolished from the mind of an adult or child. The newly emerging science of evolutionary biology explains that the human species and its nervous system developed, for the most part, when we were hunters and gatherers. Our more recent experience as farmers and manufacturers represents a mere moment at the end of our vast span of history. One feature selected for its survival value is the "fight or flight" response, in which our brain, recognizing an emergency of some sort, overrides our usual mode of functioning. Imagine you are in the woods and are surprised by a bear. For a split second you freeze, then you run for your life. Automatically, your heart rate and respiration increase, circulation is rerouted to drive necessary machinery, temporarily bypassing such activities as food digestion. Hormones are secreted, which bond to analgesic receptor sites in the nervous system. You don't notice a large, bloody gash on your arm until you reach safety, 10 minutes later. In layperson's terms, you have produced your own painkillers, more powerful than heroin or opium, to temporarily blunt your sensation and awareness of pain until the emergency is over.

Mind Over Pain

Before we had a thorough understanding of neurotransmitters, Melzack and Wall identified our ability to selectively block or diminish pain sensations. They theorized that we have a *gating mechanism*. That is, we are constituted in such a way that only so much sensory information reaches consciousness at one time. Neurotransmitters help our bodies accomplish the gating function. When pain signals are traveling from two-year-old Annie's teething gums to her brain, she does not notice the hunger pangs that often send her into a tantrum. Pain-abating chemicals are released by the gastrointestinal system to dampen the message until the more pressing problem with Annie's gums is taken care of.

We will return to the gating theory in Section IV, which covers methods of treating, alleviating, and managing pain with and without drugs.

5

Phenomenology of Pain: What Your Child Feels

Vignette: Suzie's Ill-Fitting Shoes

Two-year-old Suzie wanted a pair of patent-leather shoes like her big sister Margaret (age five). Until now, Suzie had managed to avoid wearing any shoes, and she enjoyed the freedom of running around her home barefoot. Despite her competitive spirit, Margaret was excited and gleeful watching her mom fasten the buckles on Sister's little feet. When Suzie finally rose to take her first strides in her new shoes, a sharp pinching sensation, wholly unfamiliar to her or her feet, set her howling.

Missing the point, Margaret continued to jump up and down, enjoying the look of her sister in new party shoes. Suzie promptly slapped at her sister and began to yell: "Off shoes! Shoes off!" Mom's first response to her verbally precocious two-year-old was wide-eyed surprise at her rejection of something she seemed to want. This was compounded by dismay at her taking her dissatisfaction out on her older sister (not an infrequent thing).

Suzie began crying inconsolably, which continued for some time even after the shoes were off. When Suzie calmed down, Mom asked her what was wrong with her shoes. Suzie replied: "Suzie want Margaret shoes. Suzie shoes a boo-boo."

The astute and experienced mother had to make several rapid, subtle inferences in order to discern what really happened. Only from contextual cues could she figure out that Suzie was not jealous of Margaret's bigger shoes or upset by her big sister's teasing. A careful reading of Suzie's face told her mom that a combination of pain and embarrassment was a likely cause of the tears. Evidence mounted when the two-year-old refused to try them on again, even in a larger size, for several weeks after the incident.

Later, the mother was finally able to piece together the feelings Suzie probably experienced. The pain in the toddler's toes became bound up with her disappointment at the shoes' failure to meet her expectations, the loss of her chance to look like big sister Margaret, and her mom's having allowed the pain to occur in the first place. At the moment of understanding, Mother picked Suzie up and said, "What a surprise! I thought those shoes were going to fit just right and make you feel better, and look what happened."

How did Mom give comfort to Suzie? Not by discounting her howling as a plea for attention, nor by ignoring the pain and placing undue focus on the embarrassment. She took the middle course, giving Suzie a chance to express her disappointment in whatever way she felt it. A moment of listening and a hug from Mom helped put this brief disaster in proportion for Suzie. It let her know that Mom was ready to understand how she feels *even if she could not read all of her thoughts.*

Pain is an essentially private experience. Children (and a few adults) do not understand this. They believe that Mom or Dad knows exactly how they feel; that they know where it hurts and how to make it stop. Parents and caregivers feel understandably helpless in their inability to fulfill this unreasonable expectation. Children experience this inability as a betrayal. It is a first hint that the caregiver is neither all-knowing nor all-powerful.

As adults, we cannot remember how pain felt when we were children. This is especially true for painful events that occurred when we had no words to describe them. Our knowledge that pain is subjective makes us nervous and insecure as parents. What if we get it wrong? What if we miss an important symptom? What if our child discovers that we really do not understand? What if we overreact to pain in our children? Will we be overprotective? It is clear why parents look forward to their toddlers' becoming verbal enough to describe sensations in words and analogies. Until then, parents must learn to trust that they can distinguish a cry of hunger from a cry due to diaper rash or teething.

Types of Pain Experience

What, exactly, does the pediatrician mean when he says: "This is going to hurt me more than it will hurt you?" What on earth does he have in mind when he says such a thing?

Not all pain is the same. It is impossible to directly experience your child's pain, but there is much about it you can understand. The more ready you are to understand how your child feels, the easier it will be to show empathy for his or her feelings after a bump or a scrape.

Language provides us with a rich lexicon of descriptors for pain. As adults, we can describe its onset, its intensity, and its quality, either with adjectives and adverbs or with creative analogies. Children often use more creative license to describe pain than adults, perhaps because they are less tied to conventional descriptions of things in general.

According to one study, children are apt to use words like "sore," "aching," "uncomfortable," "tiring," "horrible," and "pins and needles" most often when describing pain, unlike adults who might use "throbbing," "stabbing," "pinching," "tingling," etc., as more precise descriptors. This does *not* mean children do not experience stabbing or throbbing, rather they have not had occasion to name such feelings. Many children spontaneously use metaphors and similes, drawing from known feelings and thoughts, to describe novel painful events and experiences. In Varni, et al's study one child with a headache felt "hammers banging on my brains." Another with stomach cramps said "my tummy is twisted up in knots." It is perhaps no accident that advertisers of commercial pain relievers borrow these vivid images because of their evocative qualities.

Caregivers attempting to diagnose a child's pain can make use of metaphoric descriptions to get a good idea of where and how it hurts. In addition, children's use of language about pain is a normal part of a dialogue about how the body works and its areas of vulnerability.

Vignette: Phillip Fears a Leak

Phillip, age three, was due for a routine vaccination at his pediatrician's office. An unusually brave boy, Phillip only let out a brief yelp when the needle went into his arm. Amidst great praise from his father and from "Dr. Margaret," the physician, Phillip kept his cool until the little gauze pad was removed a few minutes later, revealing a red spot of blood. "A hole! A hole!" cried Phillip. "Get a bandage!"

Phillip took great care for the next two days not to let anyone touch the bandage. When it fell off in the bathtub on the third day, he noticed it floating and became upset all over again, calming down somewhat when he saw that his "hole" had plugged itself up after all.

Phillip's dad found his reaction a little surprising and hard to understand, until Dr. Margaret explained that children between ages two and six often have misconceptions about how the skin heals after a puncture wound. For Phillip, the body is a solid container with liquids inside, including chewed-up food, urine, and blood. A perforation in the walls of that container could cause the liquids to leak out like a water balloon with a hole in it.

Our reaction as adults to Phillip's fear is often to minimize and reassure. While this is not wrong in many cases, we could use this type of situation to correct some of the child's basic misconceptions about his or her body. Phillip's bandage can be more than just a "cork for his needle puncture" or a reminder of his fear of "leaking to death." It can also be a cue for his parents and pediatrician to remind Phillip what a wonderful capacity his body has to send special healing cells to plug up leaks. Curious children might learn that these cells are called *platelets* and become proud of the scabs that they find quickly forming over little cuts and scratches acquired during play.

How do we know how someone else's pain feels? Can we share another's pain? The question is both simple and complex. Philosophers have wrestled with this question for centuries, with widely divergent results. Some have concluded that each individual's personal experience is unique, singular, and inherently inaccessible to anyone else. We can only know another's feelings through an indirect process of logic. "If I feel such-and-such pain when I burn my finger, then, by inference, someone else might experience a similar feeling under similar circumstances." In this school of thought, empathy is nothing but a romantic idea based on an unattainable wish for closeness with our fellow creatures.

Following this type of logic, the more similar we are to a fellow creature, the fewer inferences will be necessary to make a guess about its feelings. An adult human would thus have an easy time understanding the pain of a fellow adult, a more difficult time with pain in a child or a baby, and a nearly impossible task of inferring the sensations and feelings in an animal or a plant. By similar reasoning, if a mother cannot remember exactly what it felt like the last time she fell off her tricycle (30 years ago), then she must be unable to fathom her daughter's pain today as the child cries in her lap after her first spill.

The thinkers who espouse this highly rational approach to pain and empathy dismiss the rest of the world as "naive." But rigorous adherence to logic and objectivity leaves most of us cold. A different school of thought (shared by this author) does exist. It holds that we all have a capacity to empathize with one another's feelings. We are endowed by nature with an essential ability to share one another's joy, fear, triumph, and pain.

Pain is a universal feeling. Its survival value, as discussed earlier, extends beyond its role as a signal to the injured individual. A mother whose daughter catches her finger in a doorjamb becomes viscerally agitated herself. Look at the face of a father whose son has fallen and has begun to cry. His expression is a mirror image of his boy's distress. He takes immediate action to protect him and comfort him. The healing process begins long before the wound is cleaned and bandaged. Your empathic facial expression conveys to your child that yes, indeed, it does hurt, that he or she is not alone, that you are there, that you understand, that you are (hopefully) not overwhelmed by his or her distress, and that you will stay by his or her side until the immediate danger passes.

Anxiety and Pain

All things being equal, a child with a cut or bruise, or one receiving an injection, will feel more pain if his or her nervous system is in an aroused state. A calm child—that is, one whose heart rate and respiration are at resting levels—experiences the same physical sensations as less painful.

Fear and anxiety are two emotional states that create a moderately high degree of physiological arousal. As described earlier, an individual's body and mind use this arousal mechanism to escape danger. At moderate levels of anxiety, the senses are keener. That is why we feel painful sensations more quickly and acutely in this state. An interesting paradox presents itself when anxiety levels get so high that an individual is in a state of sheer panic or terror. It seems that at very high levels of terror, pain signals are temporarily shut off, allowing time for the person in danger to escape the situation if possible.

Vignette: Billy Hates His Bath

Billy, a six-year-old child, loved to play outside and get very dirty. Like many boys his age, he'd rather stay dirty for days on end than submit to the indignity of a bath. For one thing, Billy's dad was not good at shampoos. He always managed to let soap get in Billy's eyes. Even more upset-ting, Kathy, the baby-sitter, always gave Billy a bath on Sat-urday when Mom and Dad went out. They insisted on his being clean for a weekly visit with Grandma on Sunday mornings. Kathy always scrubbed to get all of the grime out from under Billy's fingernails and toenails, which he really hated.

One Saturday, Billy decided to trick them. He came inside from a particularly muddy game of football and snuck up to his room, tore off his clothes, rolled them up in a ball, and shoved them under his bed. Mom and Dad yelled up from downstairs: "Bye, Billy, we'll be back late. Don't give Kathy a hard time, OK?" To which Billy replied breathlessly, "OK, I'll be good." Before Kathy had time to get her coat off, Billy filled the tub with about two inches of very hot water. Although he had seen this done many times before, he had never yet filled a tub without an adult's help.

Billy was nervous about getting caught, so he quickly stepped into the tub. At first he felt a funny tingling sensa-tion in his feet. He consciously interpreted this as being wrong in some way, but for a split second, it did not regis-ter as discomfort. His adrenaline was still high because of the rushing around and the intensity of the subterfuge. Then the sensation registered as burning pain. Billy screamed and, luckily for his feet, jumped quickly out of the tub before damage was very severe. Kathy rushed upstairs and found it very difficult to console Billy, who could not seem to stop crying. He kept complaining about his feet long after the burning sensation should, according to Kathy's experience, have stopped.

Ordinarily after this type of superficial exposure to hot water, Billy's feet should have felt fine after about five min-utes. Why, in this case, did Billy's feet keep hurting for an hour after the incident? Before the pain impulse traveled from Billy's feet to his brain and was finally understood as "a burning feeling in my feet," it made contact with several other brain pathways. Each pathway contributed a different layer of information and meaning to the final experience. The predominant pathway carried the pain message to the sensory cortex of the brain that underlies sensation in the feet. It told Billy, in effect, "My feet feel hot pain from the ankles down."

Some of the following additional messages might have been folded into the original message:

- "I've never been burned before and I'm afraid."

- "I'm cooked."

- "The pain will never go away."

- "My heart is pounding and I'm breathing heavily."

- "I am in danger, and Mom and Dad are not here to protect me."

- "I broke a rule about the bath and got caught."

- "What does Kathy think of me?"

- "I will be punished."

Information about Billy's heart rate; respiration; past experience or lack of it; and thoughts about his state of pain, danger, and culpability were woven into the fabric of Billy's experience of the pain in his feet. They may not have been separate feelings from the pain sensation itself. The quality, intensity, duration, and meaning of the burning sensation were modified by all of these pieces of added input.

It may not come as a surprise that a person undergoes some of the same physiological changes when he feels fear or anxiety as when he feels pain. Research has shown in many ways that a person who has a high level of anxiety (as

Billy did when sneaking upstairs) also has a lower threshold for pain. This means that the same child stepping into the same hot bath, only this time drawn by Kathy the babysitter, would likely have been less anxious, have felt less fear and anxiety, and have recovered more quickly and easily from the crisis. Would a less anxious Billy's feet hurt less? Yes. Does this mean that Billy was exaggerating his pain? *No.* Thoughts, feelings, fears, and memories are all stirred into the biochemical soup that, once cooked, comprises Billy's pain. They are not separate from the pain itself.

Could Billy also exaggerate his pain, say, to get attention from Kathy? Yes, but the histrionics many children perform when in pain are often more than mere attention-getting and should not be grounds for dismissing the intensity of your child's discomfort. Young children's pain behavior is not bound by social conventions and norms the way it is for adults. They are free to experiment with a variety of emotional and behavioral expressions for pain and other feelings as they occur. Some children rant and rave because it distracts them from the pain sensation itself. Others aim their reactions directly at their caregiver as a way of finding out how concerned they should be.

*V*ignette: *"Big Boys Don't Cry"—Pain in Social Context*

Joseph, age 12, loved to watch the big boys play basketball in the schoolyard, out in back of his apartment. They made driving layups look easy. They made fancy bounce passes and played a physical sort of game that Joseph admired. Sometimes his dad watched with him on his day off work. When Joseph wished out loud to play, his dad would say, "Play if you must, but don't come crying to me when you get a black eye going for a rebound." At five feet, five inches, Joseph was tall for his age and had become a good ball handler with his peers while practicing one-on-one. He was feeling ready for bigger challenges. During one pickup game, the boys asked Joseph if he would like to play.

The big boys were two and three years older than Joseph, and many of them towered over him at five feet ten and eleven. Joseph thought about the offer, remembering his father's admonition. What did Dad mean by "don't come crying to me"? Joseph understood his dad's words as encouragement that he should take the risk and confidence that he could handle it. The catch was, if he got hurt, Joseph would have to learn how to comfort himself in order to fit in with the big boys. Dad was saying, perhaps correctly, that pain has a different social context and a different language for expression when you play with the big boys. This fact is well understood by both Joseph and the older boys.

When Joseph entered the game, he was immediately crowded, pushed, and elbowed. He was shown who dominated the basketball court. It would take a whole season for Joseph to establish his own physical prowess. The guys would not be doing Joseph any favor by going easy on him. How else could he come to grips with the level of pain that must be tolerated from the bumps and bruises incurred in a normal afternoon of play?

Joseph's social world is much wider than two-year-old Sally's. Sally relies almost exclusively on cues from her parents and on her own physical feeling state for her repertoire of pain behavior. Joseph feels pressure to fit in and works hard to suppress any overt expression of pain so that his new friends won't think him unready to play in their game.

Being with a Child in Pain

It might be useful for the reader to review the list of pain behaviors (in Section IV) before visiting a child who is ill or in the hospital. The close observer might notice that he or she, or other visitors, are uncomfortable with the idea that there is a child feeling pain in their presence. Such people may be uncomfortable for any of the following reasons:

1. They may be so empathic that they are debilitated by their shared painful feelings.

2. They may misread the behavioral signals as anger or personal rejection by the individual in pain.

3. They may feel uncomfortable with their helplessness to alleviate the pain.

4. They may experience another's pain as a personal threat to their own well-being.

A better sense of awareness of someone in pain can help you to avoid some of the natural pitfalls that accompany the misreading of pain signals.

Factors That Influence Pain Tolerance/Pain Sensation

The foregoing vignettes help explain why some children seem to feel every little sensation as painful, while others appear impervious to all but the most violent assaults on their bodies. Careful observation of a group of children at play will enable you to distinguish the cautious from the brazen, the excitable from the calm, and those with higher from those with lower pain thresholds. Sensory and pain thresholds vary from one child to another from birth and probably run in families.

A number of physical and emotional factors influence how much and what type of pain a child might experience in a particular situation with a given physical cause.

Bigger, Louder Falls Hurt More

A child who perceives the source of his or her pain to be more serious will be more frightened and feel more acute pain. Consider Jack, for example, a nine-year-old child who fears bees and bee stings. Perhaps he has never been stung before. He does not know whether he is allergic to bee stings or not. Jack also has learned not to be so afraid of deerflies and horseflies, each of which have a fairly sharp bite. Moreover, he may know of someone who is allergic to bee stings and who has to be injected with adrenaline if he is stung.

Early one day Jack gets bitten by a deerfly, which raises a large, itchy welt on his arm. He notices the pain at the time and says, "Ouch," crying out for five seconds or so. He scratches it a bit, then goes back to playing with his friends. Later that day, Jack sees four or five bees pollinating some flowers. One accidentally gets under Jack's shirtsleeve, causing him to feel panicky. He is stung as he tries to shake the bee out of his shirt. Jack knows that the bee sting is more serious than the deerfly bite, *even though the physical sensations are similar*. Despite the similarity, the bee sting hurts much more than the deerfly bite. This time, Jack cries loudly for several minutes and does not stop until he finds his mother, who puts first-aid cream on the sting and consoles him for several more minutes.

Feelings of Pain Vary from Moment to Moment

Some pain sensations are more constant while others are more variable, waxing and waning over time. To a child, or an adult for that matter, unpredictable pain can be particularly frightening because there is no way to prepare or adjust when you do not know what is coming up next. An example of variable pain might be gastrointestinal distress that is not directly timed around meals.

If You Think You Can Control the Cause, It Will Hurt Less

A child with a sprained ankle may suffer considerable pain, even when not moving or standing up, and intense pain when he puts weight on the injured ankle. But consider the ways in which the child can have control over the timing and intensity of his pain. He can decide precisely how much weight he wants to put on the sore leg, choose when and how to move around, put ice on the ankle whenever he wishes, and take analgesic medications to reduce the swelling and the pain for periods of time. Each time he exerts some control over his pain, the child becomes more able to tolerate even severe stabs and pangs. More control means less anxiety and ultimately less pain.

Children Attend to One Main Feeling at a Time

A baby who is both hungry and teething is more likely to notice only one of the two sensations at any given time.

Similarly, an older child who is exerting herself in gymnastic exercises is less likely to feel soreness in her hands and arms while she is performing a routine. As long as her attention is focused on the practice, she is less likely to notice any other pains unless they become severe enough.

A Very Busy Child Has Less Room to Feel Pain

For a number of reasons, a child who is actively (and voluntarily) moving around despite a preexisting pain condition will be less bothered by that pain. Movement is beneficial as long as it does not cause further injury to the affected area. One reason for this is that the child uses mental energy to execute the movement, energy that would otherwise be devoted to pain behavior. Another reason is that movement activates areas in the brain that monitor body position and sensation of the areas being moved. These sensations can partially block awareness of pain.

New Hurts: More Fear— More Pain

A painful sensation that is new to the child is inherently more frightening, bewildering, and therefore more painful. Remember the first time you woke up after sleeping on top of your arm? At first you felt practically nothing except the dead weight of the seemingly foreign object hanging from your shoulder. When the blood began to rush back into the veins of that arm, you felt a disturbing sensation of pins and needles, or electrical activity, followed by intense pain. Movement made the pain worse because it increased circulation. A child experiencing this for the first time is often very disturbed by this series of sensations. His pain is exacerbated by his fear and bewilderment. Subsequent experiences of sleeping limbs are likely to be less painful.

Child's Temperament: More Sensitive Children Actually Hurt More

You intuitively know that some children just seem to feel pain more acutely than others. Such children are more excitable, sensitive, and anxious. They are also the ones who cling more tightly to Mom or Dad when among strangers. Children are born with a set of emotional characteristics, many of them inherited and all of them molded by life experience. Together these characteristics are called temperament. Your child's temperament is what makes him or her unique. We usually think of a child's temperament as something that changes very little throughout life. A child who is very sensitive, expresses emotion easily, and feels pain acutely is likely to grow up to be much the same way.

Focus of Attention: Pain? What Pain?

At any age, babies and children are capable of ignoring some pain when something else captures their attention. As you will see in Section IV, the more deeply absorbed the child's attention, the less aware he or she will be of hurting. Older children can capitalize on this ability by learning to shift attention and concentration at will. Six-year-old children can tolerate an immunization shot with some practice and coaching.

Level of Anxiety: Nervous Parent, Nervous Child, More Pain

Generally speaking, a more anxious child hurts more. Younger children and babies rely heavily on the adults around them for cues about how anxious to be. A slower heart and respiration rate comes from being physically comfortable and emotionally relaxed. A calm child's nervous system is less ready to send emergency pain signals to his brain. Absence of anxiety is not a cure for pain, but it alters its intensity.

Meaning of Pain: Social Context

When a nine-year-old gets a cramp in his calf after winning a footrace, the pain is a badge of honor. The same cramp after running away from a bully on the playground is a mark of shame. The former might be borne bravely. The latter will probably lead to tears. Pain not only signals a physical problem, it also signifies something abstract. Pain that is better understood takes on less frightening connotations. Sudden, unexpected pain, such as when a toddler falls and bumps his head, has no meaning for a moment. The child appears bewildered, looks around, realizes that he has fallen, then puts two and two together and cries. For a third grader, a sore throat could mean getting to stay home and watch TV. For her, the meaning tempers the severity of her pain.

Perception of Time: How Long Must I Endure?

Your 11-year-old has had a headache for the last half hour. She is beginning to feel as if it has always been there and it will never go away. You give her acetaminophen (the main ingredient in Tylenol) and remind her that it usually takes 10 minutes for the pills to take effect. Lo and behold, her pain gets better in three minutes. Did the Tylenol work that fast? Maybe. More likely, taking the pills gave her hope that relief was around the corner. Hope is a powerful analgesic.

Junior's Tummy Hurts More When Mommy's Around

When Mommy is present, Junior's tummyache hurts more. He wants Mommy to pick him up, comfort him, and make the tummyache go away. Junior's tummy pain is his signal to elicit pain relief.

Section III

Painful Events in a Child's Life

Specialists in fetal development believe that by the 29th week of gestation, the pain connections are ready to function. Basic avoidance reflexes are already in place, despite the fact that the womb provides a protected environment. Hypothetically, then, a shock or insult to the fetus either from the outside world or due to some process going on in the body of the fetus would be experienced as painful. Ultrasound technicians often report that introducing a catheter for amniocentesis or merely ultrasonic sound waves can occasionally cause the fetus to recoil in apparent avoidance reflex. Does the fetus feel pain or fear? We can only guess.

This section will describe painful situations encountered by most babies and children. Whenever possible, the pain will be described from the perspective of the child and an observer. We will describe the physical process underlying the pain as well as the emotional components, including fear and anxiety. We will then describe the situational factors that give the child or his or her caretaker some control over the pain.

6

Birth

When God began to create the heaven and the
earth—the earth being *unformed and void, with
darkness over the surface of the deep* and *a wind* from
God *sweeping over the water*—God said, *"let there be
light."* [Gen. 1:1–3.]

Vignette: Eva's Great Squeeze

In the womb since the beginning of forever—time and
space are fluid. Moment flows into moment. Tumbling at the
end of her tether, baby-to-be floats seamlessly from position to position. The syncopated rhythms of large and small
heartbeats float in and out of consciousness. This is the
baby's environment—continuous, hypnotic, peaceful. Now
and then, a different but familiar rhythm of gentle bounc-
ing, borne of mother's walk, comes and is gone. The com-
ings and goings of sounds and feelings begin to divide time
into now and then and about-to-be.

Now the floating slows down; the walls come closer. The
umbilicus brushes against her face and neck; and there are
pulls and tugs here and there. Baby's feet are dangling freely
with nothing to kick against. Her head begins to feel
encased. Every once in a while, the uterus contracts. The

familiar housing becomes more and more unfamiliar. Baby's nervous system responds instinctively to the unfamiliar with alarm. But alarm, too, is unfamiliar, until now. For the next several hours, alarm will become increasingly familiar. The walls come closer, and they feel harder, as the baby's head begins to drop down into the birth canal. Soon the contractions are stronger. There is a hot sensation at the top of baby's head as it is pulled, sucked up against the cervix. She has never felt "temperature" before. The heat of friction burns her wrinkling scalp. Her heart speeds up and slows down.

A nervous roller-coaster ride has begun. Another contraction. This time the friction encircles baby's face. The pressure against her eyes brings a phosphorescent light show to her mind's eye. Unable to hear Mother's heartbeat, for the first time, baby feels her first pang of loss, of separation. Another series of squeezes compresses the baby's shoulders, chest, and abdomen. Her body becomes contorted. One shoulder is down, the other shrugged to her ear. More new sensations as her soft ligaments are stretched to their limit. A rapid volley of aches, burning sensations, and sharp pains is followed by moments of serenity as baby's alarm response emits endorphins to dampen the distress.

Things speed up now. A falling sensation—Eva's first brush with gravity. As the midwife glances up at the clock, Eva is born. Blood rushes toward the center of the earth. Arms and legs flail and dangle in a cold, blowy liquid so unlike the womb: air. Sudden brightness against the eyes. This brightness is different from the phosphorescence in the birth canal. The new visual world divides into contours of light and dark. A moment of strange stillness as Eva is placed on the table. Then a coughing spasm as the midwife suctions Eva's nose and mouth. Her chest feels ready to burst forth, then a rushing of air fills Eva's lungs. The strange sound of Eva's own vocal chords vibrating in the air, crying out with each breath. A feeling of empty spaciousness engulfs her whole being. Pain, fear, distress, separation, the five senses overloaded . . .

And then, a warm surface. A soft familiar smell. The rushing of bodily sensations gives way to a soft sensation against Eva's left cheek. The vast emptiness around her body; this airy nothingness is being gently covered by the caress of Mother's big hands and body against body, skin against warm skin. Eva's heart rate and breathing are searching for a pace, a rhythm. It is easier now for a moment. Yet, the bruises on her face and eyelids smart. Her lungs burn from the cold air, even as she takes new comfort in her first cuddle. The emptiness is still there. A cry of fear is located on the lips. There's that brushing on the cheek again. Now Eva's mouth seeks the brushing feeling. The emptiness is filled! Eva's lips and palate launch into rhythmic sucking, as if to pull Mommy's breast closer and closer, inward. She sucks vigorously as sweet drops of colostrum coat the inside of her mouth. Soothing feelings sweep from Eva's mouth through her whole body as the colostrum works its magic. Pain and distress are blanketed in a cloak of euphoria. Exhausted, 10 minutes old, Eva falls into her first postnatal nap, returning her to a womb that still vividly exists in her dreams. Eva's birth pain is a memory, but it is much more than a *mere* memory, because it represents her first experience of pain after birth.

At least for now, her tumble from womb to air and gravity is her template for pain and distress. Similarly, Eva's first contact with Mother's skin and her first suck at her mother's breast is her template for relief. From that primal experience of birth, Eva has learned at least two lessons about pain relief—lessons that will serve her for her whole life. First, motherly human touch is usually associated with pain relief. Nature and evolution has seen to it that Eva will seek human touch for the rest of her life. Second, having bathed her mucous membranes in her mother's colostrum, Eva learned that with relief of pain comes potential pleasure. Eva will seek pleasure for the rest of her life unless circumstances prevent her from enjoying pleasure as babies are made to do.

Given this description of the baby's subjective experience of birth (a best guess), what do we look for in the newborn that might indicate pain or absence thereof? The most obvious sign is crying. While there is no guarantee that the newborn cries out in pain, our intuition, confirmed by our own empathic understanding of the baby's situation, suggests that when the baby stops crying it is because he or she is no longer experiencing discomfort. Parents and caregivers rely on more subtle cues to the baby's comfort level as well. Heart and respiration rate are fairly observable to the attentive eye. As the hungry newborn latches on to the breast, breathing becomes slower and more even. As a distressed baby attends to a novel or interesting noise, sensation, or odor, his or her heart rate drops. It is as if the baby's sphere of attention narrows down to one small sensation, blocking the information pathway containing pain and fear messages to the baby's brain.

7

Early Feeding, Hunger Pangs, and Colic

During a baby's first days and weeks, she and her caregivers will learn about the contrasts between distress and relief, between pain and absence of pain, and between pain and pleasure. She will come to know with gradually increasing clarity what is within her caregivers' control and what is beyond their control. This knowledge forms a foundation for what we know as emotional equilibrium. From baby's point of view, her every action, whether a burp, a movement, a gurgle, or a cry, can elicit a reaction from her caregivers. For the first three months, most painful situations will be accompanied by a great deal of parental "to-ing" and "fro-ing" in often futile, but more often successful, efforts at comforting. Even an experienced caregiver of a new baby must play a guessing game at first. It takes weeks of getting to know the baby before it becomes evident how to soothe the various discomforts.

One of the first important hurdles is to "catch" a problem such as hunger or wetness before the baby's distress goes "over the top." This is an important concept. If an adult with a headache waits to take a painkiller after the headache has reached its peak, he will find that the medicine is ineffective. The same is true with a newborn. We strive to feed the baby when her hunger is on the upswing, but not at its peak. Why? The baby's sucking machinery requires a good deal of concentration and a relatively calm frame of mind for the meal to begin. It is as if the table must be set and the candles lit before it is possible to pick up a fork. That window of time when the baby can suck requires a balance between desire and discomfort. Too much of either one results in over-the-top distress and a temporary inability to eat.

Mothers and caregivers describe two contrasting early eating patterns. One, called the "sleeper-slurper," is familiar to exhausted breast-feeding mothers who seem never to be free of the baby for more than a few minutes at a time. Twelve-week-old Josh is not a sleeper-slurper. He is the other kind. A "barracuda." Barracudas get ravenous, eat voraciously, and often sleep soundly. But woe be it to a caregiver who waits too long to feed Josh.

Vignette: Josh Gets Hungry

It is Sunday morning. Josh awakens in his carriage to a warm sun. He is in the garden with his dad, who is gratefully enjoying a moment of peace and reading the newspaper. Good husband that he is, he gave Josh's mother the morning off. Before leaving, she left careful instructions on how to heat up Josh's bottle should he wake up hungry. She even warned her husband about Josh's intense appetite. "How hungry could a baby be?" he naively thought.

Now Josh looks around. Birds are chirping. The weather is perfect. A light, warm breeze brings sweet scents to Josh's sensitive nose. Intoxicated by the kaleidoscope of color and aroma, Josh gurgles and coos. Dad sits up attentively to admire Josh's moment of alertness. Josh sees Dad's face looming overhead, blocking out the bright sunlight. His father's smile comes into focus. Josh smiles, moving his bowels in a state of admiration. Dad fumbles with the diapers. The diaper change is a struggle for both Josh and Dad. Even so, they playfully banter back and forth, a duet of coos, facial contortions, and some vigorous wriggling. Eventually Dad manages to get Josh cleaned up and changed. He is proud of himself.

Josh has been awake 15 minutes now. He feels a tightening in his now empty intestines. It is not painful, but it is insistent: a pulsating, squeezing sensation in the gut. Josh's brain has already noticed that he is hungry. Josh is no longer interested in the smells and sights and the warm breeze. In fact, they are the last things on his little mind. His food-seeking repertoire is small at this point in his short life. He thrashes his head left and right, looking for something to latch onto with his mouth. Finding the edge of his baby blanket, he sucks vigorously for half a minute. Dad is transfixed. He is proud of Josh's newfound ability to comfort himself with the blanket. Then Josh begins to fuss, slowly at first, until the tight feeling turns into painful hunger spasms. Watching intently, Dad finally gets the message. "Where is Josh's bottle of expressed milk?" he wonders out loud (a habit of many new parents).

Now the hunger pangs in Josh's belly are blended with the special kind of distress babies feel when their little world begins to disorganize. The delicate balance between the needs of Josh's belly and his brain has temporarily tipped too far in one direction. He cannot attend to both hunger and the rest of the world at the same time when he feels this way. Moreover, his crying is causing him to gulp air, bringing him even more stomach distress.

Wheeling the carriage to the kitchen, Dad finds the bottle in the refrigerator. By not taking it out a few minutes earlier, he has lost some precious time. Inexperienced as he is, Dad picks Josh up in his left arm, gently swaying him, nervously singing a wordless tune, while at the same time attempting to get the bottle warmed up in the pan of water with his right hand.

Josh is wailing. He could care less about the music and the swaying. His mouth is empty, he cannot find his thumb (he last noticed it in the carriage), and his stomach is heaving with pain. After an eternity, Josh feels the rubbery nipple against his gums. Between gasps and wails he latches, sucks for a second or two, lets go, and wails some more. Dad is worried and confused. He feels the familiar inadequacy of which babies so ably make us aware. Dad wonders out loud, "When is your mom coming back?"

Defeated, Dad stops trying to give Josh the bottle. Josh's distress from hunger has put him "over the top." He screams himself to sleep in 10 agonizing minutes. Mom gets home, catching sight of Dad, Josh still in his arms, sitting exhausted in the rocking chair. "How'd you two do with me gone?" she asks only half innocently. Dad replies, "He barely touched his bottle, even though he seemed very hungry." Now Josh wakes up again. Perhaps he is aware of Mom's return. This time the bottle is all warmed up and ready. The barracuda empties the bottle in five minutes and falls back to sleep contentedly.

What is going on in this all-too-familiar scene? Even in a baby as small as Josh, three separate systems are at work, each contributing to the pain messages getting to Josh's brain. The first message is from the stomach itself, telling the brain, "I'm empty. Feed me." Babies tend to root and suck in response to this. If bottle or breast happens to be at hand, feeding can begin. The second type of message is "Ouch, I'm crampy and gassy." This is pain and makes baby cry out. If bottle or breast is nearby, the cry is usually successful at bringing it within reach. The third type of message is more akin to adult anxiety: "My world has gone out of focus; I'm overwhelmed and scared from all this wailing, aching, and gasping." This is the part of Josh's discomfort that makes his caregivers feel helpless and anxious. The three messages combined send babies into tailspins, after which they can recover only with a brief nap and begin to cope again.

Could Josh's dad have done anything differently? Aside from being better prepared to feed Josh, no. In fact, he did the best thing he could have done under the circumstances by singing and trying to lull the baby to sleep. That way, at least Josh's problem was not compounded by an adult's anxiety. Many new parents get panicky and try "too hard" to calm the baby down with pacifiers or by walking around, only to become more frustrated when their efforts fail. A good thing to remind yourself when your baby is "over the top" is that he cannot sustain it for too long. He will soon exhaust himself and give you another chance to feed him.

Colic

A pediatrician once told me that he used to treat parents of colicky babies with a considerable amount of clinical distance. These parents, he said, were often demanding and unappreciative of his good advice and reassurance. He would tell them (correctly) that there was nothing seriously wrong with the baby, that it was probably just an irritable temperament compounded by gas in the stomach from gulping air when crying. In his effort to discourage parents from taking too much blame for the baby's behavior, he left them feeling just as helpless as the baby had made them feel in the first place. "Just be patient," the pediatrician would say, "and Baby will grow out of this in two to ten weeks."

Then he had his third child, a boy, who had a good case of colic himself. After that, the pediatrician said he became more empathic with frazzled mothers and fathers. Now he understood how a mature, experienced parent could be reduced to feelings of anxiety, inadequacy, loneliness, and even irrational thoughts of harming the baby. Unless parents have a pediatrician, family member, or friend who can listen and truly understand what it is like to live with a baby who cries constantly, they will be in for a period of real suffering.

A significant proportion of babies go through periods of severe distress during early infancy. During crying episodes, colicky babies pull their knees up, turn red-faced, refuse to suck for comfort, and may not tolerate cuddling until exhausted or asleep. These episodes can last for hours on end, day after day, for several weeks. Colic isn't a well-defined condition, and a specific treatment isn't known. Every family has its share of folk remedies for the colicky baby. Some remedies have medical merit, while others rely on "magic," the kind we use when rational methods fail us.

Some babies go through several weeks of daily crying jags that last for hours at a time. Remember that new babies experience the world primarily through the mouth and the digestive system. A day with stomach pain for a baby must be like living with a continuous earthquake. The whole world turns bad, leaving no refuge from seemingly endless distress. Baby cannot remember *not* crying, nor can he or she anticipate relief. Mom's or Dad's inability to stop the distress is in itself very upsetting. Baby's distress and parents' helplessness can feed off one another. The key to finding some peace is in the adult as much as it is in the baby.

Colicky babies appear to be suffering from intense pain. One of the biggest obstacles to caring for a baby with colic is the difficulty in accepting that fact. A baby's pain is keenly felt by his mother. Nature made us that way. So a first important step toward coping with the baby is to find ways to keep a sense of perspective and calm (see Section IV for more details). Even if a magic pill were available to cure the baby's physical discomfort, mothers and fathers would still have to help the baby recover his or her equilibrium. First, consult your pediatrician and satisfy yourself that there are no treatable medical problems accounting for the pain, crying, and distress. Second, follow the pediatrician's suggestions regarding nutrition, burping, and, if prescribed, medications. Then, in addition to those steps, think about ways to find support, comfort, and calm for yourself as well as your baby. In Section IV, see hints on how to survive the roller-coaster experience of caring for a colicky baby.

8

A Tale of Two Circumcisions

Circumcision, the removal of the foreskin of the male baby's penis, has been and continues to be the subject of controversy among parents and pediatricians alike. One of the most ancient surgical procedures, circumcision is viewed by many in modern society as a vestige of barbarism. It is not my intention to try to sway parents in one direction or another. In the end, it is mostly a personal decision between parents, often in consultation with the pediatrician. In some cases (as with Jewish tradition), religious considerations also apply. By contrasting two different surgical approaches to circumcision, I hope to illustrate some useful concepts in helping small babies cope with pain due to minor surgery. The following vignettes will contrast a hospital procedure with a traditional Jewish ritual procedure. It might be of interest that a *mohel*, a Jewish ritual circumcizer, can often be called upon to perform nonreligious circumcisions as well.

Vignette: Matthew as Surgical Patient

Matthew was born yesterday. Not that he is naive, he really *was* born yesterday. Medical insurance being what it is, there is a hurry to get him and his mother, Sue Ellen, discharged by late today or early tomorrow morning. Matthew's father, Bill, proudly demonstrates his first solo diaper change for the nurse, a strict precondition for discharge. Pulling open the paper diaper, Bill gazes down at Matthew's beautiful, perfectly formed, tiny body. Then he says "Sue Ellen, Matthew is beautiful, but he doesn't look like me." "What are you talking about?" she replies, mystified. "Well," he says, "he has many of my features, but look at his penis! I forgot all about the fact that for Matthew to look like me in that particular way, he would have to undergo surgery."

Bill had not remembered because the thought of inflicting unnecessary pain on his tiny prize, and for such a self-centered reason, was too hard to keep in his mind. Sue Ellen reassures him. "Bill," she says, "doctors have been doing this forever. They know what they're doing. Don't worry."

A few hours later, little Matthew is wheeled off to a treatment room by a pediatric resident. Having performed 25 circumcisions in his new career makes him relatively experienced at this procedure. To minimize waiting time, he has learned to get all of his surgical equipment ready before bringing in the baby. He even applies some topical anesthetic to the baby's penis and lets it take effect before beginning the procedure. That way, Matthew's pain will be much less intense. Matthew, his knees curled up to his belly, tightly swaddled in his blanket, is quietly watching the reflections on the Plexiglas wall of his crib.

Tired from his birth, Matthew is still about a half hour away from his next feeding time, and dozes off for a moment. The doctor then unwraps his blanket and removes his diaper. Matthew is startled by the gust of air on his skin. His arms and legs, not used to being free, flail about. His nurse picks him up, cradling him gently, and coos in his ear as the pediatrician quickly scrubs, dons his mask and gloves, and opens the sterile surgical pack. "Here we go," he says, trying to be cheerful for the nurse.

Matthew is placed on the table on his back. His arms and legs are gently but firmly held in place by cloth straps as the doctor attaches a special clamp to ready the foreskin for cutting. Matthew is screaming because he is cold, and his body does not like to be stretched out. His reflexes want to pull his arms and legs back into the fetal position, but they will not go. Over the next 60 seconds, Matthew's discomfort turns to rage, and he dissolves into continuous crying for the 14 minutes that follow while the doctor carefully maneuvers the scalpel around the clamp.

Thanks to the doctor's deftness, Matthew feels virtually no discomfort on his penis. With the dressing applied, the nurse quickly reswaddles Matthew. Exhausted, he falls asleep for 10 minutes. When he awakens, Mother's breast provides ready comfort.

"How'd he do?" asks Bill nervously as the nurse walks in. "Pretty routine. Matt did just fine," is the reply.

If Matthew could talk he might say, "You call it routine to take my clothes off, strap me down for 15 minutes, and let me scream like that?" Luckily for Matthew, he has the ideal temperament for this type of situation. As enraged as he was, he was quickly able to pull himself back together. Within a half hour after the procedure, he was eating and sleeping just as before. The local anesthetic will wear off

soon, but a baby heals very quickly. When occasional soreness enters Matthew's awareness, sucking on something is
sufficient to drown out the discomfort.

Vignette: Isaac Enters the Covenant

Isaac, all of eight days old, has been home nearly a week
now. He does not know it, but today is a big day for him
and his extended family. Earlier in the day, the mohel
dropped by to examine Isaac's genitals to make sure there
would be no complications. Guests begin to arrive. Food is
laid out, and there is an air of festivity. Isaac is a bit hungry because on her sister's suggestion, Isaac's mother decided
to save the next feeding for after the ceremony. Isaac's
grandmother carries him into the living room and places
him on a ritual pillow while a few prayers are said. Then he
is handed to his grandfather. With the help of the mohel,
the two men undress the baby and lay him across Grandfather's lap. (Grandfather volunteered for this honor.) A few
more rapid prayers are intoned, and the baby is held firmly
in place by his grandfather, while the mohel positions the
clamp.

With another prayer, and a nod of permission from
Isaac's young father, the mohel's scalpel does its work. He
applies the dressing to the wound and hands the baby back
to his grandmother, who quickly brings him to his mother.
Time is precious because Isaac was hungry to begin with.
His distress from the circumcision sent him into vigorous
wailing. From the time he was brought in until now, four
minutes have passed. Another half minute and Isaac would
be too upset to feed. Now he sucks hungrily. The sensations
of feeding dominate Isaac's awareness. When he next awak-

ens from his postprandial nap, he will feel occasional soreness of his penis until it heals in a day or two.

To be sure, both circumcisions were uncomfortable. But
it is a common misconception that the surgical knife causes
the most discomfort. Analgesic creams can alleviate much
of this discomfort, and as long as the wound is kept clean
as it heals, the pain dissipates quickly. Most people who have
witnessed both kinds of circumcision seem to agree that it
is the physical restraint and not the cutting itself that is the
culprit. Newborn babies do not like to be undressed, splayed
out, and physically restrained for any longer than is necessary. A baby that sucks immediately after any painful or distressing event usually calms down right away. In addition,
many believe that breast milk contains natural pain relievers. Finally, it is important to note that whenever a parent
or caregiver takes charge of and exerts influence over a distressing situation, it becomes more tolerable and less upsetting for adults and children alike.

9

Teething Pain

Most adults do not remember their baby teeth growing through their gums, although many can easily recall pain from impacted wisdom teeth during late adolescence. In their effort to show sympathy, many pediatricians say that teething pain is the next-worst pain we feel after labor pain and kidney stones. Well-intentioned comparisons like this do not add much to our understanding of what children really go through when they teethe. Scientific studies have not yet been done, for example, to measure the amount of distress children display when teething, to what extent topical or ingested remedies actually work. My grandfather advocated rubbing some bourbon (his drink of choice) directly on the gums. The problem is, who knows where the pain really is? And who knows whether the relief proffered by the bourbon is due to general sedation or local anesthesia? Another reason why more studies need to be done is that baby teeth come in anywhere from age four months onward.

As a baby gets older, he or she develops a wider repertoire of pain behavior and gradually comes to expect the caregivers to provide relief. Babies also develop the ability to point out the location of mouth pain by shoving their fist in their mouth and salivating a lot. By about the first year, many babies have vocal sounds to specifically indicate pain. (A complete discussion about pain behavior can be found in Chapter 14.)

Vignette: Charlene, the Early Teether

Charlene, six months old, has just awakened from her noontime nap. A sunny room comes into focus. Other babies are crawling on the floor or are seated in baby seats outside her crib in the day-care center. She listens to the contented sounds of cooing and gurgling, the familiar voices of her caregivers, Jessie and Melissa, and the occasional jingle of rattles. In her quiet alertness, Charlene soaks in the world like a sponge, making new sense out of every nuance of movement, sound, and sight around her. She will not be hungry for another hour or so. Her diaper is wet, but being the very absorbent kind, it does not bother her.

Jessie notices that Charlene is awake and comes over to play with her. They coo and cluck to each other for a few moments. Jessie's face is fun to look at. Her fair skin is polka-dotted with large freckles, and her face framed in a halo of flaming red hair. Jessie's voice has a soothing lilt. It makes Charlene laugh. Jessie finds Charlene's favorite toy, a soft rubber rattle with stubby fingers. She puts it in Charlene's hand, and the baby immediately brings it to her mouth. She explores its texture and flavor, and the squeaky sound that makes Jessie cringe as it rubs across Charlene's toothless gums.

After a minute of this, Charlene begins to focus on working the teether against her front upper gums. She remembers from before her nap that this was somehow satisfying, but cannot remember why. Then she feels soreness well up in her gums. It takes over her mouth and her face and soon swamps her whole being. The sights and sounds of the room become faint background to the enormous sensation. Charlene, not a big crier, lets out a screech and then chomps down hard on the teether. If she bites hard enough, she can create a sensation on her gums that drowns out the pain for a split second. Instinctively, she begins to suck vigorously on the toy. That dampens the pain for a few moments. In her mind, Charlene expects sucking to bring relief, because this action has consistently soothed other discomforts such as hunger pangs.

The colors, sounds, and patterns that were only moments ago novel and enjoyable are now somehow distorted and a bit grotesque. Between sobs, Charlene is able to make out Jessie's face, which, mirroring the distress in her own face, confirms that something is wrong in the world. Why can't Jessie make it better? Grown-ups have magical powers to make discomfort disappear. Has Jessie lost her powers? In response, Jessie picks Charlene up and cradles her against her body. She begins to hum a familiar nap-time tune. This feels a little safer, warmer. Charlene wriggles her body to snuggle closer, as if to absorb some of her caregiver's magical healing power.

For a few moments, Charlene feels better. Free of pain. The physical comfort of Jessie's touch and gentle swaying motion, along with her soothing voice and the melody, collaborate to set a cascade of antipain chemicals into action against the pain sensations from Charlene's sore gums. As Charlene begins to drop off to sleep, her left fist finds its way into her mouth. Once again, she works her fist against her sore gums. Still in Jessie's arms, Charlene feels a bit more secure. Her fist is more controllable than the rubber teething toy, and she is able to modify the pressure against her gums, stimulating a sensation that falls just shy of pain. If she bites down too hard, she gets a stabbing sensation and lets out a shriek. Jessie sings a little more and increases the rocking motion until Charlene settles back down to work on her fist and gums. As the baby is soothed, her saliva drools down her arm onto the cloth over Jessie's shoulder, and Jessie understands her own job in helping Charlene control the pain. She holds Charlene out in front of her for a moment to make eye contact. Charlene sees Jessie's new facial expression—one that says, "Things are going to get better." Now Jessie's got her magic power back.

Jessie's "power" is a subtle force here, but it is neither magical nor mysterious. She did what comes naturally to a person caring for a six-month-old. She remained tuned in to Charlene's need for comfort and calm, aware of the limits of her ability to make the pain disappear. Jessie did what she could do, which was to touch, carry, sing, and rock. She conveyed sympathy with her face, assuring Charlene that she understood and that she had hope and knowledge that the pain would pass. In effect, Jessie had faith in her own ability to handle the situation, and in Charlene's ability to make use of her comforting. She remembered that while teething pain is upsetting and distressing for the baby, it is a normal part of the development process. She also reminded herself that she had other options to rely on, such as giving Charlene something cold to suck on from the freezer or applying topical anesthetic to Charlene's gums.

In some instances, all efforts fail to achieve even a moment of comfort for a baby in distress. Jessie has learned from past experience that if she feels helpless and out of control, so will the baby. At those moments, she is never too proud to ask for help from Melissa or another caregiver. If the baby becomes too difficult to please, she might call a parent and ask if he or she has any suggestions on how to help. She could also ask the parents to stop in and try to work some of their own "magic."

Several basic principles of children's pain management are present in Charlene's case.

1. Charlene's pain is her body's natural way of getting help from adults.

2. Pain is both emotional and physical. Charlene expresses both kinds of distress, and Jessie attends to both aspects.

3. Jessie, as Charlene's usual caregiver, is aware of the baby's level of development. A six-month-old baby does not understand where the pain is coming from or why she has it. She can, however, practice some self-comforting and respond well to voice and touch messages.

4. Jessie allows Charlene to help herself as much as possible, intervening only by making the sucking toy and the baby's fist more available. Then, by picking Charlene up, Jessie creates a feeling of safety and security, enabling Charlene to continue to care for herself while at the same time offering care and comfort.

5. Analgesic medication is used only as a last resort in many cases. But it *should* be used if needed. Don't leave pain and distress untreated just because the child cannot verbally express his or her feelings.

6. Child care is demanding, so whenever feasible, it is important to call or ask others for help.

10

Immunizations and Other Painful Procedures

My first polio vaccination was a shot. Blessedly, the sugar drink was invented shortly afterward, and the only shots I needed were for measles, tetanus, and mumps. Even so, I must have been traumatized. To this day, I still have an aversion to shots. I can remember fainting on two occasions at the sight of a hypodermic needle piercing my skin when I donated blood.

As a boy, when I went to my pediatrician for shots, I remember the strong smell of the alcohol wipe, Dr. Cohen's attempts to distract my attention at the last second, and then a combined feeling of surprise and indignation. I remember even more vividly when it was my younger brother's turn. He seemed to "know" sooner than I what was in store for him. He let out a prolonged scream that was easily as piercing as the needle he was to receive. For my brother, it was clear that distraction would have been a waste of time and energy.

In those days, doctors had no uniform method to help prepare children for shots. It was not that our parents and doctors lacked concern. To the contrary, I believe they were keenly aware of how lucky we were to receive these protective vaccinations that had not existed only a few years before. As with any new medical miracle, we tend to focus first on its life- and health-saving benefits; only much later do we attend to quality-of-life issues like pain and fear. Back then, the conventional wisdom for any painful procedure was that "faster is better" (which is still true in some cases). We were to bear up as best we could while our parents rationalized that children forget bad experiences quickly.

Standards for immunization are set by the Centers for Disease Control, with endorsement from the American Academy of Pediatricians. The vast majority of physicians and public health officials agree that immunizing against certain viruses saves hundreds, if not thousands, of lives each year. Most public school systems require all children to have up-to-date vaccinations before entering class each September.

A small but outspoken minority of parents and practitioners of naturopathic medicine oppose universal immunization on the grounds that the human body is naturally equipped to fight viruses. In mounting its own natural defense against viruses, the body develops natural antibodies, which constitute a healthy immune system. (Alternative methods of health care will be discussed in Chapter 17.)

Babies begin to receive immunizations during early infancy, and periodic shots and booster shots throughout childhood. This routine medical process can cause both children and caregivers to develop fear and distrust toward doctors, toward nonaccidental pain, and toward other invasive procedures that may or may not occur in the future. But this fear and distrust need not become commonplace. Children are as resilient and forgiving as they are vulnerable and fearful. With a little help from the grown-ups in their lives, they can learn to weather these experiences with a minimum of trauma—even a sense of pride and mastery.

Each pediatrician has his or her own method of giving shots to small infants. One doctor I know has an assistant prepare the child in the treatment room. When the baby is ready, the doctor walks in, makes very brief eye contact with the baby, performs the shot, and quickly walks out! The shocked baby is then comforted by the parent and the physician's assistant, presumably associating them with relief and the doctor with pain.

Other pediatricians attempt to distract the child's attention at the moment of the injection. This is done either with visual stimuli, such as a videotaped cartoon, or by having the child sing a familiar nursery rhyme. In any case, this method may work the first time, but most children have excellent memories for painful or frightening events. The following vignette illustrates this point. (Refer also to "Phillip Fears a Leak" in Chapter 5.)

*V*ignette: Phillip Feels Betrayed

Phillip is now five. His mom, Ethel, has picked him up from kindergarten, and they are driving to Dr. Margaret's office for what has become an every-other-year vaccination. Phillip has a *sense memory* of his shot two years ago, but other than that, he associates visits to the pediatrician with blood-pressure cuffs, stethoscopes, and an occasional throat culture. A sense memory is a nonverbal mental image. Phillip knows from hearing about other kids' shots that a shot hurts, but he cannot describe the needle or the type of pain it inflicts on five-year-olds.

Nor does Phillip understand *why* he has to get a shot. The last time, he was confused by the medical reasons for the immunization, even when Dr. Margaret tried to express it in a three-year-old's language. Dr. Margaret had said that she was giving him some important medicine and that it would hurt for just a second. In Phillip's eyes, his mother had brought him to someone who seemed friendly at first, but then hurt him by making a small hole in his arm. He had felt confused and betrayed. Then, to make matters worse, the bandage was loose. Phillip was sure his blood would leak out and he would end up like a deflated cartoon character.

Phillip's sense memories are mainly of shock, betrayal, and fear of leaking. Ethel, sensing that he would be uneasy about today's visit, delays telling him until they are in the car, en route to the doctor's office. This way, she thinks, he will only worry for a half hour at most before the shot is all over with. She remembers his concern about leaking and, thinking it might still be there, explains how scabs form.

Unfortunately, she does not anticipate that his feeling of betrayal is about to erupt again. In fact, she never really understood the reason for his outbursts of rage and fear two years before. Now Phillip is steaming and he begins to protest. Ethel has to remind herself at times like this that she is Phillip's mother, and that he is her child. That helps her remain firm in preventing her five-year-old from arguing his way out of the doctor visit. As they continue driving, Ethel calmly tries to explain to her son why he needs this shot.

But Phillip is not pacified despite Ethel's efforts at reason and limits. Had he been able to understand, Phillip may have avoided compounding has own fear and anxiety over the impending visit. Now it's time to try a new tack. Ethel knows her little boy, and she is fairly sure that he'll "go ballistic" over seeing a doctor with a syringe. In the waiting room, while Phillip is distracted by the toys and the other children, Ethel peeks into Dr. Margaret's office and asks for a word with her.

Upon hearing details of Phillip's situation, Dr. Margaret reassures Ethel. She says she will give Phillip a chance to cooperate with the shot without any adult use of force and will assure him that both she and Ethel know how difficult it is for him. If, after a minute or so, it appears that he is too frightened, she will gently but firmly get the shot over with.

As Phillip walks into Dr. Margaret's office, he looks up at his mom inquiringly, as if to get a last-minute reprieve. Ethel's face betrays her resolve as well as her anticipation of what is to come. As Phillip's anxiety begins to build, Dr. Margaret goes into action. She tells Phillip that his mom will hold him in her lap and give him a tight, loving hug to help him hold very still while she administers the shot to his leg. Dr. Margaret also explains that the shot will hurt for a second, a bit like a bug bite, and then in a few seconds it won't hurt anymore.

Tears well up in Phillip's eyes. Dr. Margaret's approach has artfully dealt with Phillip's erroneous feeling that his mom is "doing this to me." Now Mom is recast in the roles of Dr. Margaret's helper and provider of motherly hugs and protection. Also, Dr. Margaret provides mother and son with a brief, accurate picture of what is to come. She has taken charge of the situation, while remaining sensitive to Ethel's and Phillip's respective needs. Phillip cries softly as Dr. Margaret wipes the leg with alcohol. His body stiffens as she counts out loud, "one, two, three." As she administers the shot, Phillip lets out a loud yelp.

Before Phillip can take his next breath, his mom tells him that she is very proud of him.

In his own mind, Phillip is still a bit peeved about his temporary loss of dignity. But he has been persuaded by Dr. Margaret's handling of the situation that his mother is not really to blame. As he pulls his pants up, Phillip puffs himself up a bit and shoots an angry glance at Dr. Margaret. (Now she is the culprit.)

How much pain did Phillip experience during his immunization? If we ask Phillip himself, he might say that it hurt a whole lot. His pain was the product of at least four factors:

1. The sensation of being physically restrained

2. The self-induced muscle tension in anticipation of the needle piercing his skin

3. The anticipatory fear upon seeing the needle and knowing that it will hurt

4. The sensation of the needle itself

It is very easy for us adults to minimize or deny the non-physical (emotional and cognitive) contributors to a child's pain. If we feel guilty for putting the child through the ordeal, we fall into the pattern of belief that the only real pain is from the mechanical effect of the needle puncturing the skin. We want to say, "Now, that wasn't so bad, was it?" or, "How brave you were!" in our efforts to convey the wish to remove the child's fear and anxiety from the equation and diminish the pain. And sure enough, children hear our wishes and learn to suppress their feelings the next time.

This well-intentioned effort to socialize children into pain-denying and pain-minimizing adults has some unfortunate by-products. Even though Phillip's arm might still ache from the shot, the severity of his discomfort can be soothed by addressing some of his thoughts and feelings. Just as fear, muscle tension, and anticipation contributed to pain from the shot, so too can comfort, muscle relaxation, and gentle words add to alleviation of pain afterward.

At home, Phillip is not yet finished coping with his ordeal. He goes to the basement and takes out two of his fiercest action figures and stages a fight with a great deal of piercing of armor, bleeding, falling down, and more fighting. What does this play have to do with his shot? Some might think that the "violence" done to Phillip has entered into his fantasy life. While that is one way of seeing it, I prefer to interpret this as a reenactment of the shot in a "safer" place under Phillip's control. By acting out, Phillip makes effective use of fantasy to gain mastery over situations where he was not in control. He uses his imagination to shift roles from the aggressor to the victim and back again. In this way, he tries to make sense of the doctor's motives, to regain some of his own lost dignity, and even to rework the role of the parent as failed savior and rescuer. If he is allowed to enact the fight again and again, he will eventually tire of the game. It is a bit like turning a three-dimensional puzzle over and over in one's hands in an attempt to try different solutions.

Amazingly, children do not need to be taught how to do this. It is their natural method of coping with the aftermath of a difficult event.

The process of playing through a painful situation is important because it enables the child to place a situation in a meaningful context. Having worked through his memory of the shot, Phillip is no longer a passive victim of what he sees as adult vindictive cruelty. Now he is part hero, part savior, and part victim. The next time he is faced with an adult exerting authority, benevolent or otherwise, he will have a richer repertoire of responses. He will feel more in charge, even when his real control is limited.

Play alone is not necessarily enough to put a painful event to rest. Once Phillip has mastered the story from a number of different angles, he may still harbor misconceptions about how and why he had to get the shot in the first place. For example, he might ask later that day whether it was punishment for some wrongdoing, or whether he was really brave. Or, he might brag that he did not cry even if he had cried. After any crisis, it is useful to debrief. In this way, the child counts on his caretakers to check the reality of his perceptions and memories of a scary event.

Thus, in answer to Phillip's boast about not crying, Ethel could take it as a cue to remind him that though he did cry, he still acted bravely by holding still, and that crying is normal and OK. She could also remind him of the big hug that helped him to feel better afterward. This kind of interchange is in no way trivial, for it helps parent and child weave and reweave the fabric of fear, danger, trust, care, and mastery each time the child is confronted with new challenges.

Vignette: Seven-Year-Old Maria Visits Family in Peru

Maria had never met her grandparents, who had stayed in Lima when her mother emigrated north to the United States. The prospect of traveling was exciting to her. Completely fearless of flying, Maria had no qualms about the trip, except, that is, for her immunizations. She would need several special shots to prepare her for crossing the border into her mother's home country. As the date for her shots approached, Maria began to ask nervous questions. Then on the day of the shots, on her way to the doctor's office, Maria tells her mother that she'd rather stay home with her father. She does not want to get those shots.

Maria had always hated needles. Her father, usually the disciplinarian of the family, was away on business, leaving her mother with the difficult task of persuading Maria to get her shots. At the doctor's office, Maria's mother realizes that she must take clear action if she wants her daughter to make the trip. First, she calls her husband and instructs him to speak to Maria authoritatively over the phone. When she puts their daughter on, he is to tell her that he fully expects her to get the shots, and that he knows that with the help of her mother and the doctor Maria can handle it. When he finally speaks to his daughter, he plays his part well, adding that both he and Maria's mother understand how difficult shots are for her. He assures her that her mother will make certain it is done in the easiest way possible.

In the examining room, Maria begins to cry. The doctor, familiar with situations like this, tells Maria that he knows how difficult it is for her. He promises to make it as quick as possible and tells her to sit in her mother's lap and let her mother help Maria hold her arm absolutely still.

Maria's mother picks up on the doctor's cues, adding that Maria can move any part of her body, except where she is getting the shot. If it becomes too hard for her to hold her arm steady, her mother says, she will help Maria as much as possible.

At the last moment, Maria tries reflexively to pull her arm away. She does not pull very hard, and her mother applies gentle but firm pressure on her arm to counteract her reflex. Maria is reassured by her mother's restraint because it is imposed in a benevolent, nonpunitive way.

Vignette: Arnie Gets a Splinter

Arnie's mom and dad are devoted to their third and youngest child, Arnie, five years old. His older brother, Stevie, and sister, Louisa, are very self-sufficient at eight and ten, respectively. Like many parents, they tend to indulge their "baby," setting fewer limits and feeling less in a rush about his achieving independence. So, when Arnie experienced the inevitable bumps and bruises that go along with rough-housing and being five years old, he would end up crying in Mom or Dad's arms and soaking up their comfort and TLC. When it came time for his shots, they were always there, hovering closely over the pediatrician, while Arnie shed buckets of tears before, during, *and* after the shots.

One summer day, Arnie and his sister Louisa are running barefoot across the back porch to play in the yard. Arnie stops short before the stairs and takes a good-sized splinter in the ball of his right foot. He feels it right away as a sting, and then as a throbbing sensation. His immediate reaction is surprise, then confusion, and a moment later, fear. The sensory pathways from Arnie's foot to his brain have sent a batch of messages. They are not quite adding up to pain until his mom pokes her head out the back door to see what is going on.

When he sees Mom, Arnie's sensations and feelings all come together. He lets out a yell, and his mother calls for his father.

Sensing the urgency in Mom's voice, Arnie raises his cries another few decibels. She walks toward him as he sits on the top step, and she attempts to regain her own composure. Arnie's response is to simultaneously reach out to his mom and to keep his foot from being examined. Mom picks Arnie up and sets him in her lap. Arnie stretches his foot as far away as possible from her reach while still holding tightly onto her neck. From Arnie's perspective, he is on the horns of a dilemma—either hold close and get comfort, or get away so they don't touch his sore foot.

His conflict intensifies when Dad arrives. Now it would be more difficult to avoid having his foot examined. Arnie understands what a splinter is. He has even observed his dad removing one from his older brother's foot after the same kind of incident a few weeks earlier. Still, the situation frightens him.

Arnie's dad understands his son's fear and goes into action. He tells his wife to calm down Arnie while he finds the tweezers. Arnie's mother takes the cue and begins to distract her son from the task at hand. A few minutes later, Arnie is rocking comfortably in her arms. Dad returns, and as he sits down, Arnie tenses again. Arnie's father has brought a mirror for Arnie to look at the splinter, and he holds it up to his son's foot. At first, Arnie averts his gaze. His dad cajoles him into taking a peek, and Arnie gets a look at the half-inch-long dark line just under the skin. His dad explains that while he removes the splinter with very clean tweezers, Mom will hold him, and they will sing some of their favorite funny songs together. He promises to get the splinter out as fast and as gently as he can.

Mom tells Arnie that they're going to get this over with when she counts to five. She promises to help hold his foot still while his dad uses the tweezers. She holds him a bit tighter and begins singing "This Old Man." By the time they are up to "he played seven," the splinter is out. Arnie has sung his way through the ordeal. Now he wants another look at his foot in the mirror. He sees the reddish line where the splinter had been and cries out again as Dad sprays some clear antiseptic on it.

When you take control of the situation, you need not remove control from your child. You can help your child retain a feeling of control by preparing him or her for the removal of the splinter and by telling the truth about how much it is likely to hurt. Another way to provide a feeling of control is to suggest that the child sing louder, the more the foot hurts.

Why were Arnie's parents so effective at helping their son stay calm and relatively cooperative? Despite their emotional indulgence of their "baby" boy, they also knew his limitations and only asked of him what he could deliver. The rest they did themselves with a team approach. Children like Arnie need their parents to take over in a benevolent way when the situation is too frightening for them to contain themselves. Other children in similar circumstances might need less control and more room to exercise autonomy.

Surgery

Vignette: In Jason's Own Best Interest

A recent true story will illustrate what can happen when attention to pain and suffering are given a backseat to life-saving medical treatment. A 13-year-old boy, Jason Stevenson (not his real name), who was very healthy and active in sports, had been recently experiencing swollen glands and cold symptoms. One morning, Jason collapsed after emerging from a shower, and he was rushed by ambulance to the local emergency room turning blue from lack of oxygen. The boy awoke several days later in the pediatric intensive care unit at a big city hospital 30 miles away. He was unable to communicate because a breathing tube had been inserted in his windpipe. He was heavily sedated to prevent him from fighting the tube or removing intravenous tubes. Four weeks later, after the breathing tube was finally removed, he would be told that a tumor had grown and compressed his windpipe, that it had been surgically removed, that he would receive several months of strong medicine that would make him sick and tired, but that overall there were high hopes of a full recovery.

When Jason could speak again he had a very short temper, low tolerance for doctors and nurses with all of their poking and prodding, a heightened sensitivity to touch, and a very low threshold for pain. From the doctor's standpoint, this was an example of a modern medical miracle, a successful physical response to a potentially fatal condition. For Jason and his family, it was nothing less than a nightmare.

From the Stevensons' perspective, painful sensitivity to touch and fearful response to invasive procedures had been subsumed to the "primary diagnosis." In such situations, patients and families are in an awkward position. Is it right to question medical professionals about pain when they are busy saving someone's life? Trying to be good patients, the Stevensons' held off raising this issue. By the time the boy's pain was finally treated, some of the trust, essential between doctor and patient, had eroded. Jason's pain had gone from acute to chronic, making it more difficult to manage.

When it finally came time to go home from the hospital, the Stevensons were fearful about being able to manage without the high-tech medical facilities. Jason's feelings of loss of control contributed directly to greater pain and sensitivity, increased suffering, and, ultimately, a prolonged recovery period.

We can learn many things from Jason's story. A message had been inadvertently conveyed to Jason and his family that his pain was not in the same league as his lymphoma, and that his complaints were exaggerated (i.e., "in his head") and relatively unimportant. A physician has nothing to lose and much to gain by treating pain problems concurrently with the primary focus of treatment. Even in life-and-death situations like Jason's, alleviating pain could contribute to better cooperation between doctor and patient, less suffering, quicker recovery, and a stronger overall bond of trust between medical professionals and those they care for.

11

Headaches

Most children complain of headaches at some time. Those who have more headaches are also more likely to complain of other physical problems such as stomach pain. Although we do not know for sure why this is, a possible explanation is that when one system in the body is not working well, other systems can become more vulnerable. Also, having any kind of pain is stressful in and of itself. Emotional stress lowers pain thresholds in the whole body. It also increases vulnerability and pain sensation.

Children's headaches are not necessarily miniature versions of adult headaches. For one thing, children describe pain differently than adults. When describing their pain, adults follow accepted social conventions. Most American adults know what is meant when words like *splitting* and *throbbing* are used to describe their pain. Commonly used metaphors were either coined or popularized by the TV commercials for aspirin. (One headache sufferer gestures with his arms: "I have a headache *this big*." In another ad, we see an image of hammers "pounding" inside a transparent skull.)

In contrast, children describe pain in idiosyncratic ways, making it difficult to determine the exact characteristics (e.g., history, severity, quality, and intensity) of the pain. For these reasons, we do not know for a fact whether children's headaches come on more or less rapidly than adult headaches, whether they are associated with situational or emotional stress, or whether they feel similar to or different from the kind of headaches adults typically suffer. Inevitably, children will learn from the adults around them how headaches are typically or conventionally described. Children who watch TV ads for painkillers may "know" a surprising amount about words and behaviors that adults associate with headaches.

Nevertheless, the two main types of headaches found in adults, migraine and tension type headaches, are also found in children. There continues to be controversy over how distinguishable the two are, and whether they merit different treatments. The traditional distinction between the two is that tension headaches originate from tension in the muscles around the head, neck, face, and jaw, whereas migraines originate from spasmodic constriction of the blood vessels surrounding the head and eyes. This distinction stems from the way the blood flows to the brain and how the cranial nerves are organized. Migraine headaches are often preceded by an aura, tend to appear on one side of the head or behind one eye, and can be accompanied by nausea and vomiting, dizziness, and sensitivity to light. Tension headaches are usually dull, diffuse, and painful on both sides of the head at the same time.

Physicians often prescribe different types of medications for the two types of headaches. For tension headaches, physicians have generally relied on acetaminophen, aspirin, or nonsteroidal anti-inflammatory drugs (NSAIDs), and move on to the more potent narcotic agents only when the others fail to provide adequate relief. For migraines, there may be less consensus on what treatments are used. While physicians are likely to begin treating migraines with the same types of drugs as tension headaches, they may also prescribe vasodilators, anticonvulsants, or tranquilizers. When either type of headache appears to become a chronic problem, antidepressant and antianxiety drugs are also helpful in managing the pain. (See Section IV for a general overview of painkilling drugs for children.)

When a child complains of a headache, adult caregivers generally make a number of quick judgments, often without even thinking about it:

- What caused it?

- Is it serious?

- Is he sick?

- Is she exaggerating or faking?

- Is this part of a pattern of pain complaints?

- Is he under some kind of stress?

- What should I do to help her?

Some parents, even if they have medical training as physicians or nurses, might have difficulty sorting out what questions to ask first, and deciding what action, if any, should be taken. A few tips offered here will be discussed further in the final section in pain assessment and intervention. The key elements are:

Observe. Watch the child's behavior for evidence of irregular activity, slowing down, sensitivity to light, change in mood, irritability, sickness, and fluctuating energy level.

Listen. Listen to the words and phrases the child spontaneously uses to describe his or her pain to you or to others.

Interact with the child. Play, talk, or otherwise engage the child's attention. Does the pain take precedence? Can the child be distracted from it? Does your providing attention help the child cope with the pain?

Elicit a description. Get the child to describe the pain in his or her own words. When did it start? Let him draw a picture of the pain, shape some clay to describe it, color a human figure in with pain-relevant colors, or point out on a doll where and how it hurts. Encourage the child to use his or her own metaphors to describe the pain. What does the child think caused the pain?

Give care and comfort. How much does the pain respond to your giving care and comfort? Is a hug and a kiss all that is needed? Does the child feel adequately cared for? Do you allow enough time to understand the child's pain as well as possible and to determine the best course of action to help alleviate that pain?

Consult a physician. Every parent has his or her own methods of handling a medical problem with or without the advice of the child's pediatrician. The availability of over-the-counter pain remedies for children would seem to encourage parents and caregivers to administer them with impunity. If your child complains of a headache and you are uncertain about its cause or whether it is a symptom of a more serious condition, it is good practice to seek professional guidance from your pediatrician. That is what he or she is there for.

12

Abdominal Pain

The intelligent stomach remembers pain and devises clever ways to avoid repeating mistakes. Recurrent Abdominal Pain (RAP) is a major cause of school absenteeism. It has been estimated that as many as 12 percent of girls and 9 percent of boys suffer from RAP. How many teachers have heard the excuse that one of their pupils stayed home from school due to a stomachache? What is going on when John or Denise wakes up on the morning of a school exam complaining of stomach cramps? Is he coming down with a stomach virus? Is her stomach pain a direct symptom of emotional distress? Did he overeat the night before as a (poor) way to cope with the anticipated test the next day? Did she *make* her stomach upset from worrying too much? Is he exaggerating some mild stomach upset as a way of avoiding a difficult school situation? Does her stomach actually become more delicate before and during big exams? Is John imitating his older sister's method of avoiding stressful situations? Is she faking, plain and simple?

Parental Attitudes

These questions are attempts on the part of parents and caregivers to make a *diagnosis* of the child's stomach problem in order to determine a course of action. If the diagnosis mainly takes into account the emotional factors, the course of action is more likely to address emotional issues. If the diagnosis emphasizes stomach acid, the course of action might be confined to antacids. Our understanding of the source of the child's pain will govern the approach we take when presented with this familiar dilemma. How much should we push the child to attend school while in pain? At what point should the child stay home? Parents are guided by their own intuition as well as their beliefs and understanding about why their children complain of stomachaches. Some believe, for example, that the stomach is a barometer for stress, that a nervous stomach is a clear indication of emotional worries. Others think that stomach upset can be caused only by food. Some might try to soothe the child with comforting words. Others call the doctor right away and offer their children medication and rest. While some parents and caregivers become easily alarmed by their children's complaints, others remain quite cool about such matters, regardless of how insistent the child's pain is.

Food as Currency for Love

The ways families relate to food and emotions stem from culture, tradition, family folklore, and even religion. Family attitudes and beliefs about food can be intimately connected to the way individuals express emotions. You may know some parents who reward their children's good behavior with food treats, or withhold dessert as punishment for not eating the main dish. You may also know families where everyone is weight-conscious and on a restricted diet. In such a situation, children may feel criticized for the food choices they make or feel guilty for eating rich foods if they do not have an ideally shaped body. In some families, the elder members may have survived periods of shortage and hunger and attempt to enforce rules to eat everything on the plate regardless of whether one's stomach is full or in pain. While such rules may rest on sound moral principles, they could adversely affect parents' and children's attitudes toward food and stomach pain.

Food is so much more than nutrition. The next time you sit at the dinner table with your family, or your friends' families, notice the emotional ambiance. Is it relaxed or tense? Is mealtime enjoyable for the family, or a time of battles over manners, nutrition, or school performance? Do the adults and children appear to enjoy eating? Are the foods presented in a thoughtful way, or tossed haphazardly onto plates? Is there a verbal ritual (religious or otherwise) in which some thanks is given for the food? Observe the way people leave the table after eating. Does anyone ever like to stay around the table to continue conversation? Do children or adults leave because they are full, because they excuse themselves, or because they develop stomach distress? In many homes, eating and its enjoyment are ways to demonstrate filial love. Mealtime is the only regular occasion for families to sit together and share experiences with one another. Children learn early on that it is important to express appreciation for the person who shopped for and prepared the evening meal. In my own home, that meant either complimenting the cook, eating heartily, or asking for seconds. A picky eater is often experienced as one who rejects the love of the cook, rather than someone who merely has narrow taste in food. If your child suddenly develops picky eating habits, however, it could be a symptom of a deeper problem.

Five-year-old Eric was brought in for a psychological consultation because he had stopped gaining weight as fast as he should. Medical examination did not reveal any explanation, so the pediatrician followed his hunch that there might be an emotional reason for Eric's change in behavior. Sure enough, after a family meeting, Eric's mother Leslie explained somewhat apologetically that her husband had lost his job earlier that year. Money was short and so was her husband's temper. The place Eric saw this happen the most was the dinner table, where his dad complained about Mom's cooking. When the complaining turned to loud arguing, Eric developed stomach pain and would leave the table. Some brief work with Leslie and her husband enabled them to settle their marital and financial woes away from Eric.

The Role of the Pediatrician

As commonplace as this situation is, medical science has much to learn about the relationship between emotional distress and stomach pain. The physician is taught to look for the most immediate cause of a complaint, working backward in time only as far as necessary to arrive at a course of treatment. If a satisfactory medical explanation can account for a painful condition, then it is often sufficient to make a diagnosis and implement a treatment plan. To bring mental processes into the picture only clouds things up. If a child's behavior appears to complicate the course of treatment, the reason for its failure is "noncompliance," according to the physician. In the narrower view of medical science, the pain is located in damaged or inflamed bodily tissue. The broader perspective locates pain not only in the tissue but also in the child's emotional and mental processes, in his or her pain-related behavior (e.g., wincing and clutching), in assistance and comfort from caregivers, and in the swallowing of medicine. Attending only to the tissue allows the pain to perpetuate itself in an unchanged environment.

Vignette: Cora's Stomach Gets a Diagnosis

Cora, age six, is brought to Dr. Held's office after missing her third consecutive day of school. Although she awakens each day feeling fine, she develops painful cramps in her stomach after breakfast with nausea but no vomiting. Dr. Held questions Cora about how the pain feels, where it hurts, and how long it lasts. He examines her stomach, finding no evidence of a physical problem. He infers that Cora has acid stomach in the morning and prescribes an antacid to be taken after breakfast. In the back of his mind, Dr. Held has also guessed that Cora is worried about school, but because he doesn't want to bring too much attention to the problem, he opts to treat the symptom only. Cora's mother is satisfied with this approach because she is eager for a fast way to get Cora back to school.

The next morning, Cora has the same upset stomach and takes the antacid, but she appears out of sorts on the way to school. Later that day, the school nurse calls to report that Cora has another stomachache.

Cora's mother takes her back to Dr. Held. Being medically conservative, he suggests altering Cora's diet to blander food. When that doesn't work, he orders a barium series to check for ulcers or other less-obvious gastric problems. He also prescribes a more potent stomach medicine in an attempt to alleviate Cora's nausea. Cora stays home again the next day, Friday, and has few complaints over the weekend. Cora's father becomes skeptical and concludes that Cora was either exaggerating or faking her pain to avoid school.

On Monday morning, he and Cora's mother send their daughter to school with a stomachache and an admonition not to complain about it. Cora is angry, confused, and afraid she will not be able to make it through the day. By noon Monday, the school nurse reports that they are bringing Cora to the local emergency room because she is now vomiting and "crying hysterically." Dr. Held meets them at the ER and immediately orders tests to rule out appendicitis, kidney infection, or intestinal blockage.

None of these tests shed new light on what has been ailing Cora, so Dr. Held finally acts on his original hunch, asking her how school has been going for her this year. Cora describes how humiliated she feels about not being able to read as well as her classmates, and how she was pushed and shoved by a bigger girl during recess when no teachers were watching.

Cora's Educated Stomach

Cora's stomach ailment was psychosomatic in the truest sense. Although she did inherit a normal but vulnerable stomach (as children, her mother and grandmother both had "delicate" stomachs), her condition worsened when she encountered fear and stress at school. Her stomach inadvertently discovered that going into spasm in the morning resulted in relaxation in the afternoon. Cora herself felt the pain in the morning and the relief in staying home. The result was that Cora and her stomach learned together that the best immediate way to get relief and avoid danger was to be distressed in the morning *and* to avoid stress in the afternoon. If either of the two pieces was missing, Cora became even more distressed and symptomatic.

It should be clear from Cora's story that *psychosomatic* does not mean *fabricated* or *exaggerated*. Our gastrointestinal tract was designed by nature to alert its owner to distressing situations to help us avoid them in the future. The complex array of nerves around the stomach are sensitive both to the stomach and the brain, enabling each organ system to learn from the other. Cora's brain tries to protect her stomach by staying home from school. Her stomach tries to protect her brain by becoming symptomatic and by bringing timely relief.

What is the best approach for Cora's parents, teachers, and doctor to take? Once we understand that her stomach is only part of the problem, we are on the way to a solution. Also part of the equation are Cora's fear of the bully, her reading difficulties, her mother's need for quick solutions, her father's distrust of Cora's complaints, and the doctor's holding back on an accurate diagnostic hunch.

Cora needed help coping with the situation so that her stomach would not have to step in to rescue her. Moreover, the earlier one intervenes, the easier it will be to avoid falling into a cyclical pattern of pain, fear, avoidance, and relief. Cora's parents and Dr. Held might have picked up on the fact that delicate stomachs run in the family. This should have signaled that Cora experiences stress through her stomach, rather than just through thoughts and feelings. That being the case, Cora's complaints should be addressed not only on the physical level, but on the mental and emotional levels as well. Cora's teachers and nurse could also be alerted to her avoidance pattern and help to nip it in the bud.

Recurrent Abdominal Pain

Occasionally, children with recurrent stomach pain continue on to develop a long-standing pattern of fear, gastrointestinal distress, and avoidance. With appropriate help from medical and mental health professionals, such children can return to functioning at 100 percent. Left unchecked, many chronic stomach conditions are likely to cause structural damage to the gastrointestinal tract. Moreover, the emotional cost of unchecked fear and avoidance patterns can be serious. It is of benefit to the child's present and future to give immediate attention to such problems.

Vignette: Mike's Recurrent Abdominal Pain

Consider, for example, Mike, a shy but likable fourth grader with few friends. Mike's parents are going through a divorce and are especially sensitive to Mike's feelings about this. Consequently, they are more lenient with him than they used to be. Mike had food allergies as an infant and was diagnosed with, among other things, lactose intolerance. His customary reaction to foods that disagreed with him was stomach cramps followed by diarrhea.

By winter break, Mike had missed an average of one to two days per week of school. The usual pattern was that he would have a few good days, then he would be sent home in the middle of the day with an attack of diarrhea. He would then stay home the following day on a restricted diet and begin again the day after that. Mike's pediatrician had made suggestions regarding diet and prescribed antidiarrhea medications, which Mike took as reliably as a fourth grader can. Once the doctor recognized that Mike's condition had gone from episodic to chronic and recurrent, he referred Mike and his parents to Dr. Marcel, a health psychologist.

Dr. Marcel got to know Mike and helped him identify aspects of school and family life that worried him. She suggested that Mike's parents seek separate counseling to learn how to protect Mike from the difficulties they were having in their divorce proceedings. She also told Mike's parents that his teachers should work with Mike's shyness by gently encouraging greater class participation. She further suggested that if he has an attack of diarrhea at school, the school nurse should make every effort to get him back to class as fast and with as little embarrassment as possible.

But Dr. Marcel was not yet done with her work. She spent several weeks getting to know Mike and what kinds of situations led to his stomach attacks. Her next task was to help Mike to get to know his own patterns better. For three weeks, Mike kept a diary of his thoughts and feelings every time he felt an attack of diarrhea coming on.

Looking at the diary together, Mike and Dr. Marcel discovered that Mike's cramps followed situations where he would have to present a topic in front of the class. Mike hated speaking in front of people. He feared humiliating himself. The cramps came with a thought that "diarrhea is sure to follow." Because Mike feared further humiliation surrounding his bowel movements, he would take the first opportunity to run to the bathroom and "relieve" his cramps on the toilet. Mike's stomach had learned that the only way to get relief from stress-related pain is to have a bowel movement. Now, in perfect accord with his own stomach, Mike actually came to believe that he must have a bowel movement as soon as possible after feeling stomach pain. The cycle was complete.

Once Mike was aware of how his stomach responded to fear and stress, he was ready to learn some new ways to take care of his stomach and his distress. (The concepts behind these methods are more fully described in Section IV.) Dr. Marcel taught Mike an exercise to make himself deeply relaxed. Mike practiced the exercise every day for two weeks. Then he used the technique to relax himself before some of the school activities that made him anxious. When he felt his stomach beginning to cramp, Mike was to think of why he felt nervous, and to remind himself that he could relax any time he wanted to. He was to tell himself that he would do fine if he just waited the cramps out.

Mike gradually learned to delay his trips to the bathroom after he felt his first urges to move his bowels. At first he would hold on for 5 to 10 minutes. Eventually he would wait 15, then 30 minutes. Once he waited 30 minutes, Mike was surprised to find that the urge to move his bowels subsided. Now, instead of the thought that "when cramps come, diarrhea is sure to follow," Mike practiced saying (and began to believe), "When cramps come, I can relax and they will pass."

With Dr. Marcel's help, Mike learned that his stomach might always be vulnerable to stress. That was, so to speak, Mike's "innate constitution." Knowing this, Mike understood that he had to take special care of his stomach. But the special care was not babying or coddling. Mike was not to avoid stress to protect his "weak" stomach. Rather, he learned that his stomach needed extra practice in coping with the normal stresses of everyday life.

To help his stomach accomplish this task, Mike identified stressful situations before they came about. Then, rather than avoid them, he relaxed himself before entering difficult situations. If he felt his stomach act up, he reminded himself to "hang in there" as much as possible instead of running away.

13

Dental Care

It is unfortunate that most adults associate the dentist with painful, invasive procedures, because this can affect their children's attitudes. We easily forget that children's visits are predominantly preventive. Children typically visit the dentist for two reasons: to get a professional cleaning and to detect signs of problems such as tooth decay. Early visits are an opportunity to instill a positive attitude toward lifelong dental and medical care. It is beneficial to seize on these opportunities when you go for routine visits, which usually do not cause the child much physical discomfort, because it can help build trust and rapport with the dentist as well as between you and the child. That way, if and when more serious dental problems arise, you can use that trust to engage the child's cooperation. Children who have well-developed, healthy ways of coping with the minor pain that accompanies some visits to the dentist will engage in better dental hygiene overall.

Pediatric Dentistry/Choosing a Dentist

The field of pediatric dentistry has arisen to fill a gap in child dental care left by general dentists who have neither the patience nor the ability to interact with a squirmy, inquisitive child. Pediatric dentists receive extensive training and experience with a wide array of children's oral and dental needs. Because they devote their professional practices to children, their success depends on their ability to understand and relate to all kinds of children. In addition to mastering the technical side of children's dental care, pediatric dentists take the time to learn and understand the specialized methods of preventing and treating pain associated with dental work in children.

A good pediatric dentist understands the value of decorating the office and treatment areas in a manner consistent with children's esthetics. Toys and activities in the waiting area help put the child in a positive frame of mind, especially when the child can continue some aspect of his chosen activity as he enters the treatment area. It is also very helpful if the receptionist and dental technicians are able to relate to children in positive ways. Good teamwork between a dentist and dental technician can be very effective in helping a child cope with anxiety about the office visit. While one is preparing equipment, the other can be interacting with the child.

Rapport Between Parents and Dentists

Just because you may have unhappy memories of your childhood visits to the dentist does not mean your child has to have the same kinds of experiences. One of the first hurdles a pediatric dentist must face is gaining the parents' trust and cooperation. While this may seem obvious, there are a number of benefits the dentist derives from his or her efforts. Children are sensitive to their parents' fears of dental care. By observing their parents' behavior on the way to the dentist, children might notice that their parents are on edge. Parents might also be a bit short-tempered, giving children a general sense that they are anticipating a bad time ahead.

One way the dentist can gain parents' trust is to prepare them for the dental visit. In reviewing the examination plan with the parents and discussing ways to prepare the child for what is to come, the dentist makes the parents a member of his or her team. With a clear purpose, parents are less anxious about the outcome. At the same time, when the child sees his mother or father working in concert with the dentist, he gets a correct impression that things are under control.

Parents and caregivers are often justifiably wary of doctors and dentists who neither know their child very well nor try very hard to get to know him. It is unrealistic for the dentist to spend an hour or two playing with your child to gain his trust, so what is the solution? The quickest route to predicting the child's needs is for the dentist to ask the parent. A five- or ten-minute telephone contact between parent and dentist is an excellent way to prepare both child and dentist for the best possible cooperation *in both directions*. Such a conversation might include the following questions from the pediatrician or dentist:

- What has the child been like in previous similar circumstances?

- What questions or concerns has the child raised about the dentist?

- Does the child know what the dentist does, how it will feel, and what he will be asked to do?

- How much does the child understand about the reason for coming to the dentist?

- What does the parent think will help the child feel safe and be cooperative?

Preparing for a Successful Exam

A good overriding principle for successfully coping with any medical or dental procedure is that a patient who actively participates in the procedure will feel more control and less distress. Active participation means different things for different children at different ages; however, the common thread is that participation encourages learning, lowers fear, and engenders cooperation.

A child who is well informed about a dental appointment can be taught to use the information to prepare for the procedure. Information without the instruction can lead to unnecessary anxiety. If the child has a plan for coping with the exam, however, he or she can enter the doctor's office with a minimum of worry. If you tend to think of a routine dental exam and cleaning as a passive experience for your child, following are a few tips that can change the emphasis to a large degree.

1. Include the child in making the phone call for the appointment.

2. Have the dentist speak to the child on the phone some time during the preparation period. At this

time, he or she can inform the child about what is planned for the appointment, and the child can ask questions.

3. Use age-appropriate language to describe and explain the exam.

4. Tell the child in advance about the appointment, but not too far in advance.

5. Normalize the experience—that is, explain that it is routine and that all children cope with this.

6. Use play, stories, books, or verbal description (depending on age level) to describe what the dentist will do, what the child will do, and what the parents will do.

7. Describe the physical surroundings that the child will see. For example, you might describe the dentist's chair and how it moves, or the "spitting sink" for rinsing the mouth.

8. Describe the sensations that the child may feel.

The electric rotary toothbrush and tooth powder are relatively easy to describe, because they involve low levels of stress or discomfort for the child. Slightly more difficult might be the taste of the dentist's rubber gloves, the sight of his goggles, the weight of a lead apron for x-rays, and the sensation of metal probes in the mouth. Even more difficult is the feeling of plaque being scraped off teeth, or having to open the mouth very wide for a long time. Most difficult is injection of anesthetic into the gums and filling cavities.

Develop and plan coping techniques with your child. The purpose of informing the child about the sensations he might feel is to give him the opportunity to prepare how to cope with them. Coping techniques include rehearsal, distraction, fantasy, guided imagery, relaxation, and control measures. (Coping techniques are discussed more fully in Chapter 15.)

Rehearsing the procedure with the child involves play-acting the dental examination. The child may play the dentist first, and then the roles may be reversed. The purpose of the rehearsal is to practice coping techniques that will be used during the examination. If the rehearsal itself engenders anxiety in the child, that means it is being done realistically. This is good. If, in the safety of home, your child can playfully elicit anxiety and then master it by using coping techniques, it will be easier to put those techniques to use in the dentist's chair.

To Prepare or Not to Prepare: Coping with "Worrywarts"

Many parents hesitate to rehearse the dentist visit with their six-year-old because he or she is a worrier. Instead, they may wait until they are on the way to the appointment before they tell the child. It is natural to want to spare a young child the ordeal of worrying about a medical or dental procedure. However, there are a number of good reasons for informing children with enough, but not too much, advance notice. Waiting until you are en route to the appointment may work the first time, but most children see the dentist regularly. If the child has an unhappy experience for which he was not prepared, he may become more resistant in subsequent visits. Worry doesn't give a child tools for coping with what is ahead.

You as parent or caregiver can help your child convert helpless anticipation into constructive preparation. Looking at the situation from the child's point of view, it seems strange to spring a doctor visit without warning. The child might wonder whether you lack confidence in his or her ability to cope. They may also consider that you feel ill-equipped to prepare them.

The way you handle the preparation is the best way to convey confidence. Note the difference between the following two approaches.

1. "Sarah, today is Friday. On Monday morning you and I are going to Dr. Stevens, the dentist. Let's practice getting our teeth examined over the weekend so we can be all ready for a good exam."

2. "Elizabeth, today is your dental appointment. Behave like a good girl and don't embarrass me, OK?"

The mother or father in the second approach sounds as if he or she has already set up negative expectations. The injunction to "be a good girl" implies that being upset about the dentist is inherently "bad." Furthermore, how is Elizabeth to be on "good" behavior at the dentist if she has no clue what "good behavior" entails? Does it mean she's not supposed to cry or be afraid? Does it require that she be polite and thank the dentist for seeing her?

Sarah's parent, on the other hand, conveys confidence in the way he or she delivers the news about the appointment. The parent can, by a choice of words and tone of voice, provide Sarah with realistic confidence in herself and in the dentist. In addition, Sarah's parent includes the idea of *active preparation* in her statement. (See Chapter 15 for a more detailed discussion.)

Filling Cavities

For many children, having a dental cavity filled may be their first uncomfortable experience with a health professional other than the pediatrician. As a parent or caregiver, you have a choice to view this with fear and foreboding or as a challenging opportunity to make a difficult experience more bearable and less frightening for your child. Increased sensitivity to children's needs on the part of pediatric dentists and thoughtful parents is the key to producing a new generation of adults who are less fearful of dentists. The following vignette illustrates some teamwork among parent, dentist, and child.

Vignette: William Gets His First Cavity Filled

Eight-year-old William was slightly small for his age and very intelligent, and his wire-rimmed glasses bespoke a bookish, well-mannered young intellectual. William's father, Al, worked as a foreman at large construction sites but had the flexibility to take time off to attend his son's dental appointments. Al was very proud of (if a bit bewildered by) William's precocious reading ability.

At William's last appointment, Dr. Driscoll found two cavities, both on the lower-left side of William's rather small mouth. At the time, Dr. Driscoll had told William that he could fill them on the following Monday after school at four o'clock.

Al knows only too well that his son is a chronic worrier. True to form, on the way home from the last appointment, William asked nervous questions about the procedure.

Al knew that entering into a lengthy discussion so long before the next appointment might be counterproductive. Instead, he suggested that they make a date to prepare for the appointment over the weekend. He also asked William to pick the time. Al did two things to offer William a sense of control over the situation. He gave William a choice of when to prepare and implied that preparation would be helpful.

At the appointed time, on Sunday afternoon, Al responded to William's concerns. But verbal reassurance and negotiation are often not enough to allay a child's worries. Many children need more concrete preparation for even a mildly invasive procedure like a filling, but neither Al nor William knew how to prepare.

Even though it was Sunday, Al decided to call Dr. Driscoll for some advice. That afternoon, Dr. Driscoll dropped off a booklet that explained and described in words and pictures everything an eight-year-old might want to know about how a cavity is filled. Al and William read it together. Now Will knew about masks, goggles, syringes, the bur, amalgam, condensers, carvers, burnishers, and polishers. He could recite the sequence of events from climbing into the dentist's chair to leaving with a red balloon. But Will was still nervous. The big question that no one had answered yet was, how would William *cope* with his fear and any incidental pain or discomfort that he might encounter?

Al Helps Will Practice Effective Coping

Al decided to begin with a couple of practice run-throughs of his son's impending filling. They made believe Will was in the dentist's chair, and Al played the part of Dr. Driscoll.

Al explained that the point of rehearsing was to help
William practice ways of feeling brave and relaxed during
the visit. He then divided the whole procedure, from beginning to end, into 10 steps. For each step, he asked his son
to think of a job he could do. During the actual procedure,
this method would enable William to count down to the finish after each job was done.

Al and William chose activities for each step and practiced them in sequence. The activities included asking the
dentist questions, manipulating some of the equipment and
controls, counting backward by sevens (distraction), tensing and relaxing muscles (muscle control and relaxation),
slow, steady breathing (relaxation), gripping Al's hand
(masking), and imagery (distraction). After their first
rehearsal, Al remarked that Will had thought of just about
every possible thing that could happen. He capitalized on
the fact that after two rehearsals, his son would get bored
with the idea of the dentist, and that boredom was a better
sentiment than worry. After the second rehearsal, Al offered
William a special reward if he was able to use most of the
coping tools that they had practiced on Sunday. Notice that
the reward is to be contingent on William's coping with fear
and pain, not on "good behavior" or absence of distress.

The Visit

On the way to Dr. Driscoll's office, Al could tell that Will
was mentally ticking off all the coping skills they had
rehearsed the night before. He correctly reminded Will that
it was OK to feel a bit nervous, and that he only expected
Will to do the best he could with what they had practiced.

On their arrival, Dr. Driscoll waved hello and beckoned
Will into one of the examining rooms. Instead of beginning

the dental work right away, he spent about 10 minutes letting Will handle some of the equipment that would be used. Will tried on some protective goggles, adjusted the height of the chair, and operated the power toothbrush. Dr. Driscoll then asked Will to tell him about his favorite astronomy book and put an outer space videotape in the VCR as he helped Will into the chair. Will spoke animatedly about planets and galaxies until the tape began.

At each step, the dentist asked Will to open his mouth as needed and prepared him for what he would feel. As he watched the tape, Will listened carefully to Dr. Driscoll, took deep breaths, and occasionally gripped the armrests when he was warned about the anesthetic needle.

Contrary to the belief of many dentists and pediatricians, the goal of distraction is not to block all awareness of an invasive procedure. Rather, its purpose is for the child to create competing awareness of nonpainful, nonfrightening images. Most children prefer to know what is being done to their bodies. They do not appreciate being "tricked" into holding still with a surprise distraction and then injected when their guard is down. That tactic may work once with a child, but runs the risk of destroying his or her trust for future medical or dental procedures.

Will's coping behaviors (asking the dentist questions, manipulating equipment, self-distraction, muscle control and relaxation, relaxation, masking, and imagery) all serve to protect him from the fear, anxiety, and loss of control that exacerbate pain. Moreover, he emerges from the visit proud of his accomplishment.

Once Will's cavities were filled, Dr. Driscoll's work was not yet all done. Will was tired, and his numb cheek felt funny. His teeth did not close properly, so Dr. Driscoll did some last-minute filing of the fillings. Each time he filed a bit, he asked Will to close his teeth and tell him how well they fit together. In this way, he emphasized Will's central role as an involved dental patient. He made sure to thank Will for being so cooperative in helping him do a perfect job. Then Dr. Driscoll asked his patient to give him a call if he had any discomfort or if he thought of some questions about his cavities.

At all times, Dr. Driscoll accorded Will the same respect as he would an adult patient. Will correctly felt that no question was too small to warrant a call. He felt grown-up in a way that was not too scary. Yes, he had a responsibility to take care of his teeth and speak to the dentist, but there were always grown-ups like his father and Dr. Driscoll in case he needed help.

Debriefing Afterward and Therapeutic Play

After painful events, both children and adults naturally relive them in words, images, and feelings. Debriefing through talk, play, or even daydreaming is helpful in coming to terms with the pain and preparing for future painful events. When Al and Will left Dr. Driscoll's office, Will's work to cope with the visit was not quite completed. As soon as children begin to develop language skills (early in the second year of life), they naturally use those skills to remember past events and to turn them over and over in their memory. In effect, children have many methods of coping with difficult events until they feel some mastery over them. Will had rehearsed before and coped well during his visit, and very little debriefing was necessary afterward. In fact, Al was more worried about Will than Will was about himself. When Al asked Will at dinnertime if he had anything to tell him about the dentist visit, Will said no and changed the subject.

If we could get inside Will's head, however, we would find him reviewing his experiences at Dr. Driscoll's office. Will might think of this as a kind of involuntary daydreaming. Why, indeed, would anyone want to remember the dentist anyway? The best answer is that he is not quite finished coping with some of the fearful and painful moments in the dentist's office. Many who study pain and trauma have found that the mind has clever ways of protecting itself from overloaded circuits. If too many painful and frightening things are happening at any given time, the mind has a way of partially switching off or tuning out the painful information. The body provides its own painkillers (see section on endorphins) to activate the "switch." This "tuning out" frees up previous energy and attention for potentially lifesaving behavior, such as fighting off predators, escaping danger, or even administering first aid. The miraculous thing is that the tuned-out information is neither lost nor forgotten, just temporarily stored away until the person can complete the job of coping with it.

For the next few days, Will's daydreams contained images of holding his mouth wide open, Dr. Driscoll counting to three before injecting local anesthetic, Will gripping the arms of the dentist's chair, and even images of the worried expression on his dad's face. As the scenes passed through Will's imagination, he reexperienced some of the fear and pain that had been "tuned out" during the dental work itself. The difference was, Will knew that the dental work was over and done with and that he was safe from pain. Each successive time Will daydreamed about the dentist, the feelings became increasingly faint until the experience was a memory.

If Will had not been lucky enough to have a patient father and a sensitive dentist this scenario might have been different. What if, with the best preparation, there had been complications and the procedures had been more uncomfortable and painful than expected? In such cases, debriefing after the visit is essential to any child's handling of the pain. Small children debrief through play. It would not be surprising to see a child between age three and seven sitting on the floor the day after the dental visit, playing "dentist" with his or her dolls or action figures.

The play may be literal, as in actually replaying the dental visit, or symbolic. Symbolic reenactments might include aggressive play aimed at inflicting and reinflicting pain and recovering in various ways, or it could involve rescuing a victim from a painful or frightening situation. This kind of play often brings raised eyebrows from parents who worry that it indicates poor coping. To the contrary, symbolic or literal reenactment of difficult events is helpful for children to come to terms with the fear and loss of control they experienced at the doctor's or dentist's. In play, the child is in full control when he or she can vicariously "reexperience" the painful events, while at the same time invent ways to cope with fear and confusion. In fact, children who undergo major surgery are encouraged by specialists to replay medical procedures in hospitals. Such children seem to recover more smoothly. It is as if they finish coping with their pain sooner by playing it out.

What can parents and caregivers do to enable children to process painful experiences through play and words? It's easier than you might think. The following rules of thumb will pave the way for most children to do the needed work.

1. Watch and listen for reenactment, pain-related play, and discussion of painful events in the hours and days

after a painful event. Learn to recognize it and appreciate it for its adaptive value.

2. Do not laugh off or otherwise minimize children's symbolic play or debriefing questions or comments.

3. If the child calls for it, get involved in the discussion of the child's experiences and memories of a painful dental visit. Your memory for the events can help remove any misconceptions the child might develop as he or she recalls them.

4. For smaller children, make toys or books available for the child to use as props as he or she replays painful events.

Traumatic Pain Memories

Many parents ask whether pain endured by infants and children will harm them in later life. As mentioned earlier, there are groups of people who oppose routine circumcision of the infant male's penis on the grounds that the pain will create a permanent traumatic memory in the child. While there is no scientific evidence to support such concerns, there certainly are extreme cases, when painful events are traumatic (as in an accident involving danger and severe injury), when it may be too difficult for some children to cope in the normal ways outlined above. In these instances, children might have nightmares or vivid memories of frightening events called "flashbacks." These images seem to intrude into awareness at unwanted times and with surprising intensity.

Flashbacks or traumatic dreams may occur more frequently in the days immediately following a trauma, then with decreasing frequency and intensity as time passes. In some cases, children are able to block painful memories from conscious awareness until some time later—months and even years in more rare circumstances. Recovery of painful memories has been the subject of legal controversy. Human memory is highly subjective and unreliable, making it questionable for testimony in a court of law. But this does not negate the extensive evidence for the ability of the human mind to divide awareness between dangerous, painful thoughts and all other thoughts. Survivors of war atrocities often are forced to bury their memories of those events for extended periods until they feel safe enough to disclose the facts to others.

Mouth Pain

Why does your child seem to "exaggerate" the severity of a sore throat, gum pain, a canker sore, or a toothache? Pain is pain and we have said that we must assume it hurts if you or a child says it hurts. This must remain a fundamental assumption, ensuring trust between the comforter and the comforted. But we also know from experience that different pains in different parts of the body *feel* differently. Remember that the nervous system represents the various areas of the body unequally across the corresponding sensory receptive areas of the brain's cortex. A great deal of information comes from the hands, mouth, eyes, and ears, whereas comparatively little information comes from the surface of the torso and the legs.

Section IV

How to Alleviate Your Child's Pain

Parents and other adults who care for children know many ways of soothing children's daily or occasional bouts with pain. This section provides a more systematic approach to assessing and alleviating a child's pain. Specific pain syndromes are described to illustrate some methods of caring, but the approaches are by no means limited to any specific health condition.

One can imagine, empathize with, even feel another's pain. Many parents will readily agree. But the question remains: how do you know exactly how badly your child hurts? In small children, pain and distress are very difficult to distinguish. A good example of this occurs when your five-year-old gets a routine immunization. By that age, he has learned to expect some pain and begins to protest as you enter the examining room. You, the nurse, and the doctor all gang up on the frightened child and hold his arms and legs down "for his own good." After a brief struggle, the doctor injects the vaccine, and your child is bawling. The nurse may make a comment afterward that "it didn't hurt that much, now did it?" You feel instinctively offended by this remark. Why? Because you know that your child is crying from distress more than from the needle itself. A rule of thumb is, *the younger the child, the more difficult it is to distinguish pain from distress.*

Younger children have a limited vocabulary for expressing different types of pain and discomfort, as well as a narrow range of past experience with such feelings. As children develop language skills, they are also acquiring an increased understanding of the differences among their various emotional states. By the time a child is four years old, the verbalization "ouch, that hurts" begins to replace simple crying out. By putting words to the feelings, the child shows us a new-found ability to share abstract information about his pain with others around him. He is saying, in effect, "not only do I feel pain, but I am using a word that indicates that the problem is indeed pain and not sadness or some other type of distress." Parents and teachers also know that a child who can put strong feelings into words is a child with greater control over his impulses. Such children make and keep friends more easily, read social situations more accurately, and, very important, recover from distressing situations more quickly.

14

Assessing Your Child's Pain: In Context

Assessment and Diagnosis

Before you can respond to your child's physical pain symptoms, you must ascertain that your child is indeed hurting somewhere, somehow. Learning about your child's pain can be impressionistic. That is, you often guess based on a feeling in the pit of your stomach, what you have seen and heard, and what you know from past experience. Most parents and caregivers are fairly confident in their ability to know how much their child is in pain. However, there are times when a child's symptoms are more ambiguous, when there are several contributors to the child's discomfort and to his or her ability to express that to the caregiver.

At these times, a more careful *assessment* of the child's pain can lead to a more effective response. Assessment is the *questioning* process that your doctor goes through before arriving at a conclusion (or guess) as to what is causing the problem. After making a complete assessment, the physician will make a decision about the underlying problem. Your doctor calls this decision a *diagnosis*. It is important to note here that we are not suggesting that you take over your doctor's role in diagnosing medical problems in your child. You do, however, have a special role in your ability to describe the symptoms. In fact, your doctor relies heavily on the combination of your child's own descriptions and your observational skills in his or her effort to reach a diagnosis. From now on when the word "assessment" is used, we will be referring to the evaluation of the symptoms, behaviors, situations, and feelings associated with pain, and not necessarily their underlying cause.

Medical assessment includes a combination of looking, listening, testing, manipulating, and, in some rare cases, even smelling! Your pediatrician usually begins the assessment with what is called a "presenting problem." This is the first obvious sign to you that something is amiss with your child. At the beginning of a visit to the doctor, the child answers some simple questions about the presenting problem to give the doctor a better description of what is ailing him or her. From this discussion, the pediatrician notes the child's "chief complaint." Often the chief complaint and the presenting problem are sufficient to arrive at a diagnosis.

The pediatrician continues the assessment with a physical examination. The doctor might osculate (tap or percuss) the body to look for types of congestion, listen with a stethoscope, test for fever with a thermometer, check reflexes with a rubber hammer, and time heart rate and respiration by taking the pulse and looking at a watch. For a child in pain, the exam would continue with the physician probing affected areas of the child's body with his or her hands while asking the child to say how and where it hurts. In the case of a bone or joint, the doctor might gently manipulate the joint to ascertain range of movement.

If the doctor is still not certain about the problem, he or she will continue the assessment further until there is enough information to reach a conclusion and begin some sort of treatment. If more information is needed, the physician might do one of the following three things.

1. The doctor might suggest that the parents and child continue to observe the symptoms and see if they get worse or better over time. Medications may or may not be recommended at this point. Painkillers are often prescribed for conditions for which there is no definitive diagnosis.

2. He or she might order some more technical tests to investigate the causes of the complaints and symptoms. Typical tests might include laboratory analysis of blood and urine samples, or scans of affected parts of the body using instruments such as x-rays, CT scans, scans using special dyes for contrast, or magnetic resonance imaging (MRI). The results of these scans shed light on problems involving bone fractures, intestinal blockages, sinus congestion, and vascular problems, any one of which can cause pain symptoms.

3. Occasionally the tests reveal a problem that goes beyond the general expertise of the pediatrician. In

this case, the pediatrician sends the child to a specialist, whose role is to continue the assessment, complete the diagnosis, and either treat the problem himself or herself or refer the child's care back to the primary pediatrician. There is a different type of pediatric specialist for almost any ailment you can think of. Some of the more common specialized doctors a pediatrician might call upon include: an orthopedist, for problems related to bones; a gastroenterologist, for problems related to the stomach and intestines; a neurologist, for problems with headaches, dizziness, or sudden changes in the sensations or motor coordination; and an ear, nose, and throat specialist for chronic ear, sinus, or nasal problems.

Vignette: Mom Assesses Tom's Problem

Eight-year-old Tom returns from a day at summer camp with a sad face. He walks through the front door slightly bent over, joins Ellen in the kitchen, and lowers himself to a chair, wearing a very sour face. Ellen suspects something is wrong from the tone of Tom's voice, from his unusual way of moving slowly and gingerly, and from the situation. Usually, after camp, Tom runs to play with his favorite computer game. Not this time. Ellen begins to probe by asking Tom what's wrong and whether he had a bad day at camp. When Tom answers in monosyllables, his mother knows that something is not right and begins to explore the problem further. She wants to find out if her son is upset about something specific that happened at camp or, perhaps, if he is not feeling well.

The ABCs of Understanding Your Child's Pain

There is a logical, systematic, and commonsense approach to assessing your child's pain. The simple mnemonic (memory) device "A-B-C" can remind you to observe your child's pain behavior in the context of what went on immediately before the pain started, and what happens afterward.

Looking for Patterns, Phase I: Antecedents

"A" refers to *antecedents*. When does your child first experience the pain? Any aspect of the situation may be relevant. Is it a time of physical activity, emotional stress, or interpersonal conflict? Is the child doing schoolwork before each episode of stomach pain? Are his siblings arguing over the TV? Is dinner about to be served when she gets a migraine?

For a situation to qualify as an antecedent, there should be some sort of pattern to its timing in relation to the pain. If pain only follows once or twice after a particular situation, it may be a coincidence. If pain commonly occurs with a specific situation, it is time to be suspicious of a relationship between the two.

The connection does not need to be obvious. For example, parents often assume that children who develop pain symptoms just before school are having problems at or on the way to school. Often, the pain turns out to be associated with *leaving home*! Even when pain comes on due to a sudden, unexpected accident, context is a crucial part of understanding and responding to it. If your one-year-old is struggling to walk across the room for the first or second time unassisted and falls down, you understand his pain in the context of his efforts. The pain is probably not severe, so your response to it is not overblown.

Looking for Patterns, Phase II: Behaviors

The general expression "ouch" and Tom's listlessness in the earlier vignette are both called *pain behavior*. Pain behavior is any verbal or nonverbal expression of pain. Some types of pain behavior are more blatant than others. A good coach observes his athletes very carefully for indications of pain or injury, so they don't hurt themselves more by playing sports with an untreated injury. We might say that in addition to being very observant, a good coach, like a good parent, has a great deal of empathy for his athletes' feelings. Following are some examples of pain behavior:

- crying or moaning

- clenching teeth

- panting or gasping

- clutching an area that hurts

- limping or favoring an area

- tensing muscles around a sore area

- decreased athletic performance

- rubbing, licking, or stroking a sore area

- closing eyes

- requesting or taking analgesic medication

- curling up into a fetal position

- becoming irritable or edgy

- displaying a constricted range of emotion

- verbalizing the pain

- fainting

- asking for medical attention

The above behaviors can be found in adults *or* children. In addition to these, children may display the following:

- becoming unusually quiet or mute

- clinging to the caregiver

- kicking or flailing

- screaming

- running, hiding, or asking to leave a situation

- bladder or bowel incontinence

- avoidance of toileting

- aggressive behavior (e.g., biting)

- vomiting

Younger children tend to make greater use of nonverbal signs and signals to indicate pain. As noted in earlier chapters, the more loudly and clearly a child expresses distress, the more likely he or she will receive a quick response from caregiving adults, and the less likely the child will come to serious harm.

What are you to make of any particular behavior when your child appears to be in pain? A five-year-old boy might grimace whether he is dragging a heavy toy across the floor or pulling a bandage off of his arm. More subtle is the distinction between a quiet, pensive six-year-old who is pre-occupied with her school homework and a girl the same age who becomes a bit withdrawn when she has a headache. For a parent with good observational skills, an understanding of the context, and good communication with the child, the distinction becomes fairly easy.

Vignette: Mom Assesses Tom's Problem

Why make a distinction between pain and pain behavior? At first glance it might seem that there is no difference between pain and the outward signs and symbols of that pain. Pain behaviors offer you a rich opportunity for observing your child's level of discomfort.

Compare two types of useful information gained by Ellen as she and her son, Tom, walk to baseball practice. Tom moves more slowly than usual, with his arms hanging at his sides, a lack of bounce in his step, and his face a bit drawn. She asks him what's wrong, and he tells her that his shoulder hurts and that he's afraid they won't let him pitch. Despite efforts by Ellen to get him to describe the pain more fully and Tom's sincere wish to cooperate with her, he cannot offer a very clear description of what is ailing his shoulder. Yet, it is clear from his pain behavior that something is wrong.

Ellen probably has little chance of obtaining an accurate reading of Tom's ailment unless she takes her son's description and his pain behavior into account. Some parents might overreact and decide from the scant information so far that Tom should definitely not play ball. This is addressed more fully in the following section.

Looking for Patterns, Phase III: Consequences

Careful observation of your child's pain condition includes a close look at the *consequences* of his or her pain behavior. Consequences indicate more than the conventional idea of reward and punishment. Children learn very quickly from their surroundings. They like to behave in ways that get a reaction from people around them. Furthermore, as children develop, they learn to behave in new ways to bring new responses. For example, a baby's cooing noise elicits all kinds of interesting facial expressions from adults. A three-year-old's cry elicits a range of emotional and behavioral responses from her parents, friends, and caregivers. Preverbal babies and toddlers eventually learn that crying with pain brings hugs and kisses (and a close inspection for trouble). It is not hard to imagine, then, how a baby could stumble onto the fact that crying without pain also brings hugs and kisses, at least until the grown-ups catch on. An adult caring for a small infant will almost always give the baby the benefit of the doubt that its cry should be answered with comforting. Eventually, however, the caregiver might wonder whether he or she is missing some sign of discomfort, or whether the baby just wants to be held.

Mothers and fathers often ask the pediatrician, "Why does my baby cry so much in the afternoon?" In response, the doctor could inquire about the *antecedents* to the crying episodes. Suppose the antecedent is often a nap. The crying itself would define the baby's pain *behavior*. What are the *consequences*? The baby gets picked up, cuddled, and carried around, sung to, diaper changed, and so on, until he either exhausts himself and falls back to sleep or becomes interested in something other than being carried. If you consistently pick up your baby every time he or she awakens from a nap and cries, your baby is likely to learn to cry every time he or she wakes from that afternoon nap.

Now, there is nothing particularly wrong with this pattern unless you get tired of feeling obligated to respond in the same way every time. Eventually, caregivers observe that when a baby is not picked up right away, he or she often learns how to calm himself or herself down. This kind of learning is a natural part of growth and development in the relationship between baby and caregiver. A healthy child will protest loudly the first few times his or her cries are "ignored," then he or she will discover his or her thumb, the blanket, a pattern of light to look at, or a rattle to shake. In effect, what you have done is to remove a consequence— you have initiated a change in the pattern of your response to the child's pain behavior. In this particular case, the baby's change in behavior does not necessarily mean that he or she is in less pain. To be more precise, the baby has associated being picked up with the cessation of distress. By not attending to the child right away, the caregiver allows that association to naturally fade out.

Vignette: Margot's Diaper Rash

Margot, age four years and one month, has long been ready to be out of diapers. She understands what is expected of her. She has the bladder control. She is dry and diaperless all day but insists on wearing a nighttime diaper even though she usually awakens in a dry state. She does not like the feeling of waking up wet in the morning, and she knows that her mom and dad would like her to lose the diapers once and for all. Why does she cling to the diapers, her parents wonder? Even more puzzling is her habit of waking up dry and wetting her diaper while lying in bed!

Several weeks of this pattern eventually lead to Margot's developing a painful diaper rash. Margot's diaper rash is not terribly serious, but it makes her uncomfortable sitting for long periods of time. One typical place she complains of the soreness is at the dinner table. This complaint often leads to Margot's excusing herself from the table and getting a bath, which she greatly enjoys. Leaving the table gives Margot temporary relief of the discomfort of sitting, as well as from having to observe table manners.

Looking at Margot's rash objectively, it is evident that her complaints of pain (her pain behavior) are reliably followed by relatively pleasant consequences (a bath). Does this mean that Margot should not be allowed to soothe her rash in the bathtub? No. The value of understanding the role of the tub as a pleasant consequence is a bit more subtle. The enjoyment of a bath as a time to play may inadvertently have become associated with urinating in the diaper! The trick will be to try to separate in Margot's mind the use of the diaper from the enjoyment of the tub. She should be bathed at regular times, regardless of rash discomfort, and, perhaps to drive the point home, as a reward for waking up with a dry diaper. This way a new, positive association is created with the bath and toilet training.

More About Assessment

So, now you ascertain that your child is in pain due to some problem somewhere in his or her body. You have a good understanding of the context of your child's pain behavior. You have analyzed the antecedent events, consequences, and feelings that surround the child's pain. Perhaps you are about to bring your child to the pediatrician's office.

Your nine-year-old girl, Nancy, is rocking back and forth cradling her stomach in her arms, and you ask her to tell you how she would like to describe the problem to Dr. Richards. You tell your daughter that it would help most if the doctor could hear about the problem in Nancy's own words. You and your daughter are trying to get at what is called the *phenomenology* of her pain: what it feels like, looks like, and seems like. When behavioral observation and analysis are not enough, you need information directly from the horse's mouth.

Nancy is not big on verbal communication, so it is necessary to find other avenues to help her convey her problem to Dr. Richards. Many of the following are approaches developed by pain specialists in pediatric clinics. All of these methods are easy to employ at home or at your pediatrician's office.

Using drawings. Used in the right way, a child's drawings can provide a window into the subjective experience of his or her physical and emotional world. For this reason, drawing is an activity used by child psychotherapists to understand and communicate with children. Many children are unwilling or unable to give verbal expression to strong feelings and sensations. They may not have the vocabulary to describe their sensations or may be too afraid to put them into words. Drawing is used as an expressive therapy, a way for children to express feelings that have not been put into words. To make this possible, the adult speaks in a nondirective way, suggesting that the child draw anything he or she wants to. Variations on this approach involve adding specific focus to the instruction to draw, such as the following:

- "How about drawing your pain"

- "Draw a picture of how your pain feels"

- "Use the colors in your picture to show me where and how it hurts"

- "Show me your tummyache with crayons"

The virtue of these kinds of instructions is that they are as nondirective as possible. It is important to avoid giving the child a sense that he or she must perform up to some standard for you. Thus, you should avoid saying things like, "Show me how well you can draw," or "Draw an exact representation of . . ." If this were possible, the child could probably use words and gestures just as well.

A slightly more structured version that I use when under pressure to get a quick diagnosis is to provide the child with a picture of the outline of a child. I might also supply the child with a box of crayons, and I ask that he or she color in the body to "show me where and how it hurts." I might offer further cues to help the child select colors to differentiate different types of sensations.

Using dolls (or action figures). Many children have a distorted and inaccurate mental image of the way their bodies are arranged in space. Ask a five-year-old to draw a human figure, and the legs will often stick right out of the head. This happens because a five-year-old sees his feet when he looks down. He sees a foreshortened image of his body that is too difficult to depict in three-dimensional space.

Children also have irrational fears about their bodies. When you ask a child to point to his or her body to show you where it hurts, the child may be reluctant for fear that you will further irritate the area or, worse, discover something horrible like a hole or a gash. For these reasons, children find it easier and less threatening to point to the part of the doll's body that represents the place where the child is experiencing discomfort. You might think the doll should be proportioned like the human body, but this is not always necessary. I have had success getting children to describe their pain symptoms by pointing to stuffed teddy bears.

Dolls and puppets make very effective tools for easing a child's fears and talking about a physical or emotional problem. Left to their own devices, often with no adult prompting, children reenact their pain problem in doll play. "Playing doctor" is an important way for children to achieve emotional mastery over fearful experiences, memories, and situations. You, as an adult, can engage with the child in his or her doll play and get valuable emotional (if not factual) information about what is wrong.

Another reason why doll or puppet play is helpful is that children do not always understand pain as a medical problem in the way adults do. For a child, his sore elbow is part of a narrative—a story that started when he tried to climb on his big brother's bike when his brother was not looking. His hurt is less a matter of a bruised bone and scraped skin than it is a story of risk, excitement, fear, and guilt. With a doll or action figure as a prop, it is not difficult to engage a child in the retelling of the tale, complete with dramatic buildup and denouement. It is natural for a concerned adult to ask a child to skip the story and get to the end so he or she can "assess the damage." But for the child the damage is more than just physical and the pain is more than the scrape and the bruise. He also feels pain from his guilty feelings about using his brother's bike without permission, from falling down, from being unable to control the bike, and from having to admit all these things to his parents. All these feelings are capable of changing the meaning this boy attaches to the aching and stinging sensations he is receiving from his elbow.

Remember, as a parent or caregiver, you do not have to play the role of doctor with your child. You use doll play not to get at the specific physical location of a pain but rather to help your child get help from you. In contrast to the way a physician interviews the child, doll play and drawing help the child by broadening the scope of the discussion beyond the wound. While the physician remains detached and outside of the story, a parent knows that he or she is often *part* of the story. For example, a five-year-old might have one doll kiss the other doll on the spot where the pain is. You might say that this is the child's way of "mothering himself" through the pain crisis. The child casts his mother in a key role in a narrative reenactment of the pain story. In doing so, he rehearses the roles of comforter and comforted. Very young children can be seen playing and replaying scenarios like this for hours, or as long as it takes to master the emotional experience of whatever caused the pain.

To employ this method with your child, first ask the child to pick a favorite doll, ideally one that the child is familiar with, then ask the child how the doll is feeling. Most children appreciate grown-ups who understand that dolls can have feelings just like people. This type of questioning often brings a hint of a smile even to a very unhappy child's face. At this point, ask the child either if the doll knows where he or she hurts, or if the doll itself has any aches and pains. Then ask the child if the doll's aches are in the same place as the child's, worse or better, higher or lower, or any other comparisons that might be of use. If the child says something like, "That's silly; the doll doesn't hurt—I do," your next response can be, "Then, show me on the doll how and where your body hurts." With time and a little patience, you might ask the child to have the doll help tell the story of how the hurt started. From the story, you will get hints of what the child thinks was the cause of the pain. This can be valuable information, even if not factual.

If the child does not want to tell you things directly, then ask if the doll can do some of the talking. If the doll is too shy to speak directly with a human being, introduce a second doll or a puppet to conduct the interview. All of these actions can jump-start the child's natural tendency to tell and retell painful or exciting events through imaginative play. By joining in this play, you are accomplishing much more than an assessment of how and where it hurts. You are helping the child begin the process of healing.

Learning about anatomy and bodily functions. As you work with drawings and doll play with your child, you can use the opportunity to correct his or her misconceptions about how the human body is put together and how it works. A good example of this is the child who has stomach pains due to constipation. It is not uncommon for children between three and seven to be fearful of making bowel movements. These fears can develop for both rational and irrational reasons. Occasional pain that accompanies some bowel movements can cause children anxiety and lead them to avoid or delay bowel movements, creating constipation and yet more pain. Other children appear to become confused about the origin and destination of their stools. They might be afraid that flushing them down the toilet is a dangerous way of losing a part of their bodies. Still others are fearful of being flushed down themselves.

Even though a child might fear the mechanics of bowel movements, he or she can at the same time be fascinated by the intricacies of "plumbing"—both internal and external. That is why I ask children who complain of stomachaches if they have an idea of what might be going on "in there." Most children have only vague notions about how the stomach (or the house plumbing system) works. To help them understand, we draw pictures of food going into the mouth, getting chewed up and digested, being absorbed into the body as nutrients, and then being expelled as waste. Children particularly enjoy drawing the plumbing system, as the waste is carried from the house through the sewage system to waste treatment plants and beyond. Even when the children already know about these things from school, the act of reviewing the process with a sympathetic adult can be a good opportunity to temper fears with knowledge and understanding.

Developing a pain vocabulary. Drawing and doll play are helpful for all the reasons described so far and for an additional reason. By getting your child to communicate with you about how he or she feels, you are helping him or her to develop a vocabulary for describing a wide variety of feelings and sensations. A child with a good working vocabulary for feelings, sensations, and emotions is said to be *psychologically minded*. This kind of mind-set or ability is the root of a child's empathy for the feelings of other children as well. Psychological mindedness comes in handy when picking friends, resolving conflicts, and even achieving social popularity. Psychology also has a word to describe those who are unable to understand feelings and emotions, *alexithymia*.

Of what use is emotional language to a child in pain? The ability to express painful emotions is good for both child and caregiver. For the child, words are available to voice feelings and, by making them understood, to let go of them. By expressing feelings of pain and distress in the present, with all their dramatic force, a child can potentially free himself of later intrusive memories of those feelings. Studies have shown that when a person experiences shock from an auto accident and is unable to process feelings in a normal way, that person can be vulnerable to later emotional experiences where the "lost" or unexpressed feelings intrude into awareness, even years later. This is thought to explain the genesis of posttraumatic stress.

When the child is in pain and is able to express his or her emotions immediately, the caregiver is much better prepared to offer help and support. It is also valuable for the caregiver to know how seriously to take a child's complaints. A verbal exchange between a child and an adult can serve a dual purpose of conveying the problem to the adult and teaching the child some pain vocabulary:

Vignette: Evan (Age Four) Learns Some Pain Vocabulary

Evan: Mommy, I don't feel good.

Mom: What is it, honey?

Evan: I feel yucky.

Mom: Tell me more about that yucky feeling. How else does it feel?

Evan: Something hurts (he points toward his head).

Mom: You have a headache?

Evan: Yeah. What's that?

Mom: It's when you have a hurt somewhere in your head. Can you show me where with your finger?

Evan: It's in there (pointing to his left temple). Get it out, Mommy. (He starts crying.)

Mom: Let's see what kind of hurt it is. How big is the hurt? (Evan gestures, showing a space of about 12 inches between his two hands.) Does it make any noise? (He shakes his head no.) What kind of animal would make that kind of hurt?

Evan: An elephant sitting on my head.

Mom: My goodness. Is it sitting on your whole head, or just on that side? (He points to his left ear.) How does your ear feel?

Evan: Like crinkly paper in there. I want you to scratch it.

Evan's mother did a good job of eliciting a lot of helpful, descriptive material from Evan. It is by no means necessary to make an accurate diagnosis. Remember that you are not trying to replace the pediatrician, only gathering useful descriptive information to assess the situation. By asking more or less open-ended questions (as opposed to yes/no), Evan's mother helped him to develop spontaneous metaphors for a rich description of a possible earache or headache. Further, her own empathic way of speaking elicited a natural cry and enabled her to give him some immediate comfort.

Keeping in mind that a parent's job is to emphasize expression over precision, you can help your child enrich his "pain/feeling vocabulary" with use of color, shape, and metaphor. Pains can be red or orange, pointy or bumpy, scratchy or achy, loud or quiet, big or little. As you become familiar with your child's feeling language, you are better able to distinguish new problems from old, and the familiar from the unfamiliar. A pain/feeling vocabulary need not be limited to words. As your child expresses his or her feelings and sensations in drawings, doll play, movement, and even facial expression, you gradually come to share a common set of definitions used for different feelings.

Calibrating and using a pain scale. If you have a child whose pain comes and goes, such as recurrent headaches or abdominal pain, create and calibrate a scale for measuring the intensity of your child's pain. You might think of this as an easy concept for an adult to grasp, but it may be difficult for some children. I have found that children as young as three years of age can understand some kind of pain scale. A pain scale helps children describe how severe their discomfort is in comparison with some standard. Typically that standard is based on a known painful experience against which the child can compare a new sensation or pain.

To begin, ask your child to describe the worst hurt he or she has ever had. Most kids recall a shot, falling off a bike, or getting a finger caught in a door. That description serves as the upper anchor for the scale. On a scale of one to five, getting the finger caught might be a "five." (Scales with greater than five points are too difficult for most children.) Then ask the child to describe the mildest hurt he or she can think of. Children might refer to something like getting fingernails manicured, or getting hair brushed. Call that type of hurt a "one." If possible, try to determine a type of hurt that falls close to the middle between the least and most severe types of pain described. Call that one a "three." Now you have a calibrated scale. The scale enables you and your child to track the progress of a discomfort over time.

You need not be disconcerted by the fact that one child's "three" on a five-point pain scale may be very different from another child's "three." The significance of any child's rating is that it gives you a basis of comparison for other pains in that same child at other times. Suppose it is 5:00 P.M. Your child has a headache that he gives a "four" on the pain scale. He takes an analgesic, and you ask him at 6:00 P.M. how his head feels. He might say that he feels better, with his pain rating down to a "two." What you have just done is to start a pain/treatment diary, a very valuable tool to use when your child has either recurrent or chronic pain problems that require repeated attention.

Variants on Pain Scales

The Faces Scale was developed by Lonnie Zeltzer and Samuel LeBarron for preschoolers to rate their pain in a reliable way for a comparison over time. The scale works the same way as a numerical one-to-five scale, with the face at the far left indicating no pain, and the face to the far right indicating the most pain the child has ever felt.

For older children (eight years and up), pain scales can be constructed like a thermometer, with a "low temperature" signifying low levels of pain, and "higher temperatures" as more severe pain. Remember that all scales must be calibrated so that they mean the same thing to the child each time he or she uses them.

Keeping a Pain Diary

Suppose your daughter, Carlie, has frequent headaches, stomachaches, and other assorted aches and pains. You have

spoken with your friends about Carlie's complaints and they
seem to do little more than shrug their shoulders. You have
phoned the pediatrician twice. The first time he asked Carlie to get on the phone to describe her symptoms, which she
was very willing to do in detail. The second time, the pediatrician asked you if you could see any pattern to Carlie's
pain. In the earlier section on assessment, pain behavior
was discussed in the context of its antecedents and consequences. As you think about Carlie's complaints over the past .
week, you wonder to yourself whether Carlie's pain has anything to do with food, school worries, a virus, or perhaps
something serious that the doctor should know about. Carlie seems to have pain episodes at various times of the day
and week, both at home and at school. Why can't you find
any pattern? Are there no reliable antecedents or consequences to Carlie's pain? Does Carlie become uncomfortable at completely random times?

This is a common dilemma. Because Carlie has frequent
complaints of pain in various parts of her body, we might
think of her as having a "pain syndrome," a constellation of
symptoms that are tied together by some common thread.

In this situation, a pain diary can be an indispensable
tool for clarifying the problem. Many people are resistant
to keeping a diary at first. Reasons may include a fear that
it devotes unnecessary attention to the pain, or that it won't
add much to what is already self-evident about the problem
at hand. Some people simply complain that there is no time
to keep a diary. It is necessary to overcome these obstacles
for a diary to be a useful tool. It is often helpful, therefore,
to explain why a diary is suggested.

There are many ways to compile a pain diary, ranging
from very simple to very involved, depending on what you
are looking for. What does a pain diary add to your own

"live" observations of Carlie's pain complaints and behavior? Several things. A pain diary is a *prospective* way of observing behavior. That means you do not have to rely on memory of past events. Memory clouds painful past events. That is our mind's way of protecting us—of allowing us to concentrate on the present. Even those of us with a fairly accurate memory for past events tend to distort past *painful* events. A pain diary is a tool for improving your memory of painful events to help provide you and your pediatrician with useful information for diagnosis and treatment.

Carlie's pediatrician suggests that she keep a diary over the next seven days. That way, he will see an example of how her painful episodes occur in a wide variety of contexts, including school and weekdays, nighttime, and daytime. In her diary, with some help from her parents, Carlie will keep track of the following aspects of her symptoms:

- date and time of onset of symptom

- duration (date and time of relief from symptom)

- a description of the symptom (headache, stomachache, etc.)

- location of symptom (using drawings or words)

- severity of symptom (number on a calibrated scale)

It is important to make the diary easy to use. Otherwise, the quality of the information will not be good enough for you to draw any conclusions. The easiest thing to do is to make a calendar of the coming week and place headings within each day of the calendar corresponding to the five categories above. All Carlie has to do is fill in the blanks.

CARLIE'S PAIN DIARY								
SUNDAY								
	8AM	10AM	NOON	2PM	4PM	6PM	8PM	10PM SLEEP
Pain Onset/End	xx			xx	xx	xx		
Description	headache				stomachache			
Severity (1 to 5)	2	4	4	5	2	1	5	5 5 1
Location	eyes				lower abdomen			

Looking at Carlie's record of Sunday's symptoms, we observe that she had two separate pain episodes, each lasting several hours, each reaching a "five" rating at some time during the episode. Her record of subsequent days will be compared against Sunday to see if there is any meaningful pattern. For example, perhaps Carlie gets headaches seven days a week, but gets stomach problems only on weekends. If that is true, then it might be useful to obtain more detailed information on the following weekend in order to better understand the antecedents and consequences of her stomach pain episodes.

What if the diary still does not uncover the reasons for the pain? Then a more detailed diary can help solve the mystery. Returning to the concept of antecedents, behaviors, and consequences, we can ask Carlie to write down some information about where she was, what she was doing, and what she was feeling and thinking before, during, and after her pain episodes. The more detailed version of Carlie's pain diary can help her, her parents, and her pediatrician make a better guess at some of the factors contributing to her episodes of discomfort. If, for example,

Carlie's stomach pain arose only on Sundays when Aunt Bertha would visit on the way home from church, Carlie might not "put two and two together" and realize that there could be a relationship between the visit and the stomachache.

Here is an example of a more detailed diary Carlie kept on the following Sunday. She was instructed to pay attention to her thoughts, feelings, and actions before, during, and after her stomachache episode.

CARLIE'S PAIN DIARY—THE FOLLOWING WEEK							
SUNDAY							
	8AM 10AM NOON 2PM 4PM 6PM 8PM SLEEP						
Stomachache Onset/End	start 3 5 4 4 2 end						
Situations	Aunt Bertha arrives dinner						
Thoughts/Feelings	dread no appetite						
Behavior	hide in bedroom sneak snack						

What can Carlie and her parents gather from her new diary? A few guesses might include the following.

1. Carlie's stomach is upset because of her distress over having to visit with Aunt Bertha. It would be worth finding out what about her aunt's visits is so upsetting to her!

2. Hiding, Carlie avoids Bertha, whom she blames for her stomachache.

3. Missing dinner is rewarding because she is relieved of having to see Bertha.

4. Missing dinner contributes to her stomach distress as well.

5. Carlie's clandestine snack before bedtime might serve as a reward for her successfully having avoided Bertha. This perpetuates the cycle of pain and avoidance for Bertha's future visits.

At no time should Carlie's pain be minimized. A better understanding of the context of her stomach upset can help guide Carlie toward a more adaptive way of handling Bertha's visits. Chapter 15 will offer some ways to help Carlie avoid her stomachache without necessarily having to avoid Bertha.

15

How to Make
Your Child Feel Better

Now that you know how to recognize pain in your child, understand it in context, empathize with it, and talk about it easily, you are ready to lay on the proverbial healing hands. The fable about Androcles and the Lion, in which a mouse removes a painful thorn from the lion's paw, strikes a powerful chord in all of us. Here is a little mouse, vulnerable to becoming lunch-in-one-bite for a lion, many times its size. The reader is moved not merely by his bravery, but also by his empathy for the lion's pain. It was for this empathy that the lion indebted himself to the mouse.

Chapter 5 explained why we have empathy and how it helps us understand other people's feelings. Empathy is one of those natural aspects of the way people relate to one another that are usually taken for granted—that is, unless you are in pain and someone doesn't show empathy. A child will tell you that a lack of empathy will make the pain hurt more. Conversely, the first step in alleviating your child's pain is to express your natural tendency to be empathic. Before you rush to the medicine cabinet, remember that showing a child empathy can be an essential catalyst for any medicine.

Empathy and Comforting

Many parents ask whether empathy can be learned. Folk wisdom asserts that you are born with it as with a talent for music. But with most psychological character traits, the origin of empathy lies both in genes *and* in learning. Even if you think of yourself as having a tough skin or lacking empathy, do not count yourself out as a potential empathizer.

Following are a few methods you can use to show empathy for a child.

1. Try to imagine what it would be like in the child's position.

2. Reflect or mirror the child's facial expression in your own face. If a child is crying, you need not cry, but an empathic adult shows an appropriate degree of concern, sadness, or pain.

3. If possible, touch the child. Make yourself available for the physical comfort that comes with a hug, a kiss, or merely touching the affected area.

4. Listen to what the child is saying. Acknowledge both the content and the emotion in the child's voice. In this way, you tell the child that it is OK to talk about his pain.

5. Believe the child's complaints unless there is very clear reason not to. Children have very perceptive antennae for detecting insincerity. Take the child's complaint at face value. Do not attempt to minimize the child's distress by saying things like, "It's not so bad, is it?"

Talk and Play (It's OK to Cry)

Pain is essentially a private experience, but telling others (making the private public) can bring relief. Children learn early that expressing pain brings loving and caring from parents—up to a point. Children hide pain from their parents if they believe the pain to be a punishment for some wrongdoing, or if they fear that disclosure might lead to frightening visits to the doctor and possible painful medical procedures. When you encourage your child to talk about a painful event, you enable him or her to relive the event in the safety of your comforting presence. An example of this process is given in the section on dental procedures.

Children have a natural tendency to talk about a scary event that has occurred in the recent past. If they are not interrupted, children act out scary events and reenact them, much to the consternation of the adults around them. Children are more likely to do this if they feel safe and in the presence of an empathic listener. This kind of talk and play is a child's way of mastering a situation or feeling over which they had little control before. Once a child has achieved that feeling of mastery over his fearful memory, he will spontaneously stop reliving the event.

How do you get your child to talk or play himself or herself through a painful event? Here are a few pointers. Even though most young children will spontaneously reenact difficult experiences, many older children (especially boys) have already learned unspoken cultural or familial "rules" against expression of emotions. If your youngster is already "trained" to tough it out, your best bet is to initiate talking yourself. You might ask him to tell you about what is ailing him, and then not be satisfied with a merely factual report. Look at the difference between eight-year-old

Jeff's first and second passes at telling his father about a sports injury:

Dad: Why are you limping like that, Son?

Jeff: Well, I went for a layup playing basketball, and when I landed, another boy's leg got in the way of my knee, and it got bruised.

Dad: Tell me more about how it happened. Were you in a game? Did you have to stop playing? How did the whole thing make you feel?

Jeff: I was *so* angry that he got in my way! I really wanted to make that point, and now look at my leg. I can hardly walk. (He begins to cry.)

Dad: You really were upset about that, weren't you?"

Perhaps Jeff did not expect his father to encourage him to express himself, but once he got the green light, he was more than willing to let out some of his pent-up feelings.

Boys and girls ages two-and-a-half to seven often express themselves through symbolic play. To facilitate this, provide the child with play activities that enable him or her to use imagination. Children who receive medical care that involves pain can benefit by "playing doctor." Girls find it easy to use their dolls, and boys often use superheroes or action figures to act out the ordeals they have been through.

Sometimes it is not easy to recognize when a child is working things through with play. By getting down on your hands and knees and trying to become a part of the play, you can often find out. You might find a three-year-old girl alternately poking a doll with a pretend hypodermic needle, and then comforting it by singing and cradling it in her arms. Or, you might find a boy attacking one action figure with another, and then bringing them both to the army medic. He might give the toy soldiers tips on how to cope, perhaps the same ones you have given before. He'll need to keep offering those coping tips to his action figures until he believes they have value for himself.

A child who has been given the opportunity to prepare for a painful procedure at the dentist's or doctor's office will be all the more ready and equipped to do the "work" of playing or talking it through afterward. The best example of this is when you show your child how an injection will be done with his toy doctor kit before leaving for the appointment with the pediatrician. Doing this sets a precedent for the child to use the same toys to retell the narrative after it is over. The adult who originally does the preparation work is most likely to be honored with participating in the after play.

The talk and play approach also applies to spontaneous events like a bump on the head or a stubbed toe. Parents find it comes naturally to pick up a newly walking toddler after the child falls down, and to give comfort even when it is not called for. Soon, however, we begin to let the child learn to comfort himself or herself before we rush in for the rescue. Should we move quickly or hesitate when a six-year-old boy falls off his new bike? There is a middle ground between the two responses. You can be attentive, available, and caring without being unnecessarily intrusive. If your six-year-old wants to brush himself off and get back in the saddle, more power to him! But if he knows that you are ready and willing to give a comforting hug, he might find more strength to brush himself off the next time. So, the paradox is, if Suzie knows she is allowed to cry, then she may not always *need* to cry.

Talk and Play Through Traumatic Events

The same principles apply to extremely frightening situations. If a child is hurt in an automobile accident or receives a severe dog bite, he or she is said to be traumatized. We explained earlier in the book why some children have temporary amnesia for traumas. By blocking the danger from consciousness (or dissociating), the child can avoid panic and delay the feeling of pain until he or she reaches safety. The memory of the traumatic event is stored separately from the pain. Until the child talks about the event, he or she is not likely to associate the pain with the event. Thinking of the event would not evoke memory of the pain, nor will feeling the pain evoke memory of the event.

Nevertheless, children and adults naturally want to talk about a traumatic event if the right conditions are present: a feeling of safety, an empathic listener, and a belief that he or she will receive comfort. Some medical professionals and laypeople still believe that it is often better to let sleeping dogs lie. However, the prevailing view is that talking about the trauma enables a child to reintegrate his feelings with his memories of the event. In theory, a failure to do so risks the development of posttraumatic stress. Children can become disabled by unwanted memories of a frightening event repeatedly intruding into consciousness. Other consequences of prematurely burying the memory include irritability, fearfulness, and disturbed sleep. Professionally trained therapists are available in many areas to help children use language and expressive play to prevent or treat posttraumatic stress symptoms. Research shows that the sooner a child talks about a painful or frightening event, the less likely he or she will develop an emotional problem.

Touch for Comfort: The Laying On of Hands

There is something magical about human touch. Biblical stories from the Jewish and Christian traditions recount miraculous healing with the laying on of hands. The followers of Mary Baker Eddy formed the Christian Scientist Church around a deep abiding belief in the power of faith to heal the sick. Faith healers are valued members of spiritual cultures the world over. Yet the world of natural science scoffs at faith healing. Many worry that gullible believers will forgo needed medical treatment in favor of quackery. Nevertheless, even educated, scientifically minded people can experience the healing benefit of human touch. Especially children.

Healing and curing are not the same. We expect modern medicine to cure illness. This is a tall order. A number of illnesses remain incurable, including rheumatoid arthritis, diabetes, many forms of cancer, multiple sclerosis, AIDS, and many others. Medicine can control some of the symptoms and, in many cases, prolong life. Painkillers and other treatments diminish discomfort. But modern medicine sometimes stops short of *healing*. When a healing hand touches an ailing person, his illness may not go away, but his suffering might be eased. Even otherwise healthy babies languishing in overcrowded orphanages have a high death rate due to a lack of being handled and touched. Some possible explanations for this are discussed earlier in the book.

This section suggests ways to use healing touch and perhaps to get more out of it than you expect. Empathically touch a child in pain and you alleviate the pain through the magic of comfort. It is not even necessary for the child to be a "believer" for him or her to feel some of the effect of

a healing touch. To a hurting child, you as a caring adult
have the power of healing touch if you choose to use it. To
do so involves accepting your role as caregiver and the heavy
responsibility that goes with it. Your child looks up to you
and expects you to protect him or her from danger and to
comfort fear and distress whenever they arise.

These days, adults have become more cautious about
touching other people's children. With heightened sensitivity and concern about child abuse, adults are correctly reluctant to physically handle other people's children. This can
put schoolteachers and day-care workers at somewhat of a
disadvantage when a child is in need of physical support.
Many preschools and day-care centers now have written
guidelines and training programs on the appropriate uses of
physical contact between adults and children. As a rule of
thumb, in the absence of a written policy, it is worthwhile
to discuss this issue with the parents of the children you care
for, and with your coworkers. (Some preschools, for example, have rules against children sitting in teachers' laps.) For
the sake of discussion, we will assume that you have permission to provide human touch as comfort to children in
your care when they become hurt or distressed.

The need for the comforting touch of a caregiver's hand
is naturally present in children. Children who seem not to
need this have had it "learned out of them" by caregivers who
did not routinely use touch as a means of expression and
comfort. (This is probably true regardless of whether corporal punishment is used.) If you think about it, a child does
not need you to explain why you are giving him or her a
shoulder to lean on, or a comforting touch on the arm. It is
a self-evident part of human communication. Adults with
severe illnesses describe the feeling of what it is like when
friends and family stop touching them as much. It is as if
they are being removed from normal social intercourse.

Though children cannot describe this as well, they feel the same things. A hurting child simply wants the comfort of a thoughtful, empathic adult.

What makes a touch comforting? First, the intention. If you accidentally lay a hand on a child's shoulder after he has fallen off his bicycle, he is not very likely to experience that hand as a comfort. If you intend to give comfort through touch, it will occur in the context of comforting feelings and words. You will mean for the touch to give comfort. Your intention to touch is similar in some ways to tone of voice. Think of two contrasting ways to say, "I hope your leg doesn't hurt." One version might be sarcastic and the other sincere, leaving the listener with two distinctly different feelings.

It is not always so easy to achieve the right intention when offering comfort to a child. Think, for example, of the situation where a three-year-old runs into traffic. His father reacts, instinctively grabbing him by the arm and lifting him back to the sidewalk so quickly that the child is frightened and physically in pain from being dragged off the street. To make matters more difficult, the father shouts angrily at the child before calming himself down enough to realize the child is too young to really understand. At some point he sees that the child's arm hurts and wants to give comfort. He picks up the child, and the boy arches away in anger and confusion. Neither father nor child was emotionally ready to give or receive comfort at that moment. After a few more minutes, the father can compose himself enough to focus completely on his son's feelings. Only then can his touch have the intention to comfort.

Touch should be appropriate to the circumstances. Many children do not want to lose face in front of their friends. As unfortunate as this is, a team coach with presence of mind can remove the hurt child from the situation and lend a healing touch out of the line of vision of his or her teammates.

The way you touch a child should be proportionate to the type of pain he or she is suffering. Think of how you would handle your two-year-old after she has pinched her finger in a drawer. You would first check to see that the finger itself is not severely injured, then cradle the child in your arms while she cries. You might rock her gently and sing softly to her to help her recompose herself and soak up your comforting intentions. You might never actually need to touch her painful finger. Your rocking, cradling, and singing is all clearly intended to start her on the way to healing.

The prototypical example of comforting through touch is breast-feeding. Being held by mother and sucking at the breast overrides any and all other sensations for the baby. Baby boys who are circumcised on the eighth day of life are instantly comforted by the breast mere seconds after the surgery. After the feeding ends, most babies sleep for a while, giving the skin a chance to begin its healing process.

Not all parents are equally comfortable using touch to impart comfort, and not all children are temperamentally suited to being touched. Some babies recoil from the most well-intentioned caress. Some children's skin is very sensitive to touch and experience touch as a tickle. These children are highly aroused, rather than relaxed, by touch. Some pain conditions also can increase a child's sensitivity to touch and temperature.

Some children are very particular about where they are touched, who touches them, and why. Just because a child is hurt or in pain does not necessarily mean that he or she wants comfort in that particular way. For these reasons, the watchword for touch is *awareness*. Touch and caress your baby as long as the baby likes it. If the child recoils or is not calmed as you intend, try something else, such as movement or sound. When you reach out to comfort your older (verbal) child, watch for the reaction as you approach him or her. Keep your eyes, ears, and heart open to the possibility that being handled is not on the child's agenda at that moment. If comforting touch is right for the moment, with the right awareness, both you and the child will know it.

Touch comes in many forms. As noted above, breast-feeding newborns are comforted by the warmth and naturalness of skin-to-skin contact with the mother as well as by oral sensations from sucking. As baby develops, he or she begins to enjoy nuzzling, caressing, and stroking with the gentle hand of the caregiver. Mothers and fathers do this instinctively as they develop natural closeness with their babies. Usually this type of playful and sensual touching forms the cornerstone of baby-to-parent conversation. I touch you, you coo back at me. You cry, I pick you up and interact with you. Babies eventually come to associate touching, stroking, kissing, and nursing with purely pleasurable interaction with Mom or Dad. Then, when something painful occurs, you pick up the baby and do that very same kind of touching, kissing and comforting, with perhaps a slightly different tone of voice.

You want your baby to know that you understand that he or she hurts, and that you believe your comfort will soothe the pain. If playful and affectionate touch is not a major part of a parent's repertoire with the baby, touch will be less effective in an emergency. Adoptive parents learn quickly how comfortable or uncomfortable their adopted baby is with human touch. If the baby is not used to being handled very often, or worse, if he had been handled roughly before the adoption, it will take time and patience to reeducate him to enjoy physical contact.

Rocking and swaying your baby is another way to comfort him or her. We do this naturally because it works! Why? Rocking mimics the motion experienced by babies in the womb, where they were always happy and comfortable.

Swaying rhythmically creates an oscillating visual and auditory experience which lulls babies into a hypnotic state of attention to those experiences. (We'll discuss hypnosis later in this chapter.) Rocking motion may be simply an effective distraction for babies. Besides, while they are being rocked, babies are probably getting kissed, hugged, and spoken to in a soothing voice.

Massage Relieves Tension, Eases Pain

Massage can be an effective way to comfort a baby or a child. Books are available on baby massage techniques. They are mostly aimed at easing muscle tension, improving blood circulation, and, according to those who understand it, "rebalancing energy fields." If you have had a massage as an adult, you know that the right kind of stroking and pressure can be very calming and relaxing. Some even find that it is just about the only way they can really relax and let go. As with other kinds of touch, if massage is already a part of your repertoire, it will be more effective as a pain reliever. If your baby or toddler is used to receiving a pleasurable, relaxing massage on a regular basis, then he or she will be more receptive to receiving the pain-killing effect when the need arises.

You need not be an expert to massage your baby. As with adults, massage works best in a warm, dimly lit room. If baby is comfortable with her clothes off, she will enjoy your working your hands from the midline of the body out to the extremities, using a mild oil as a lubricant. (Calendula oil, which works well, can be found in health food stores.) As you stroke the baby's torso, arms, and legs, talk or sing softly. Even very small babies show clear delight, cooing, smiling, and laughing.

Babies who endure long bouts of colic, and who are difficult to hold and cuddle when in pain (see Chapter 7, "Early Feeding, Hunger Pangs, and Colic") are good candidates for massage when they are not in severe distress. Massaging your colicky baby is a good way of making a positive connection after hours and days of stress. You can use this special time to teach the baby how to relax himself, how to receive therapeutic touch, and how to associate your voice with something other than your desperate efforts to stop his crying.

Some older children also like massage, especially if they have been getting massages all along. Older boys and girls learn body awareness mostly through physical and athletic activity. They can enhance bodily awareness through massage by learning how muscles get too tight, overextended, or just plain tired. That way, children can learn to avoid overtaxing themselves in training for sports. An eighth grader, for example, might get a back and leg massage from a trainer after a long-distance race. The purpose of the trainer's massage would be to alleviate pain from muscle tension and spasms after intense exertion. In the process, the eighth grader will come to learn and understand the consequences of that kind of exertion for his leg muscles and adjust his training accordingly.

Magic and Ritual in Everyday Healing

Transitional Objects: Baby Comforts Herself

Soft, fuzzy things like blankets, lambskins, and stuffed animals provide critical comfort. Babies and toddlers often have a special object that is never far from reach. It can be a blanket, a corner of a blanket, a stuffed animal, a pacifier, even his or her own thumb. Once the baby has selected a special object (called a *transitional object* by developmentalists), he or she rarely switches allegiance to a new object. Some pop psychologists have thought it unhealthy for babies to rely on a transitional object, however, a majority would describe it as a natural stage of emotional growth.

You may have observed a baby or a toddler sucking his thumb while stroking his cheek or lip with the soft corner of his special blanket. He is re-creating the pleasant feelings and emotions once available only from mother's breast. Transitional objects help babies and young children make a transition from total reliance on mother's touch for comfort to transitional reliance on the special object, until the toddler is able to develop his own internal emotional resources to comfort himself. With the help of his special soft blanket or toy, a toddler learns to remember what Mommy feels like in her absence. It is no accident that babies' first words are often the name they use to call their transitional object. Like the blanket, words are also babies' tools for remembering and envisioning people and objects that are not in the line of vision.

In the case of inanimate objects, it is the baby that must maintain the contact even if you initiate it. Suppose your baby wakes up in the night with what seems like digestive distress. You know that it will be a while before the distress resolves itself, and you cannot spend the next hour carrying the baby around your house. You can help the baby find his transitional object, empowering him to comfort himself. I have found that as long as a living, breathing parent is within sight or reach, the transitional object is only second best. This method works best if the adult makes himself scarce long enough for the baby to find comfort for himself. If you consistently offer your child his transitional object in times of distress, he will eventually come to look for it or ask for it himself. This kind of behavior marks the early stages of self-reliance and ability to stay on an even keel.

Kissing the Hurts Better: Mom, the Ritual Healer

Kissing is, of course, a special kind of touching. Each culture has its own customs and traditions about kissing. For some, kissing is a sexual act between consenting adults. For others, kissing is done more with noses than with lips. In Western society, parents kiss children as a way of showing love and affection. We use kissing in ritualistic ways as well. When we kiss each other hello or good-bye, we are imbuing the kissing ritual with a kind of magical power. It's as if to say, "If we kiss good-bye, nothing bad can happen while we are apart," or "Let's make sure that an act of affection is our last expression before we part, in case something bad happens." And, to affirm our superstition, we kiss hello, symbolically saying thank-you to the magic good-bye kiss for keeping us safe.

When Mom kisses Sadie's bruised elbow, she is performing a healing ritual. What makes the kiss a ritual? Several things. Sadie runs to her mom because she is supposed to be her protector and caretaker. While Mom is not always able to prevent Sadie from falling and bruising her elbow, she is at least able to make sure the pain goes away. Ever since Sadie can remember, whenever she fell down or got hurt, Mom would say something like, "Ohhh, does that hurt? Let Mommy kiss it better." Then she would ceremoniously place a special kind of kiss on the bruised area, saying, "There, that ought to do it." After that, Mom would pick Sadie up and hold her, letting her cry a while, maybe distract her with a song, and start her on some new activity to help her forget her bruise. While each specific situation may have been different, the basic ritual has a set of fixed elements:

- running to Mom

- hearing her expressions of empathy

- getting a ceremonial, make-it-better kiss

- receiving some comfort and distraction

After much experience with this ritual, Sadie correctly believes in its magic. The kiss makes it better because her mom knows it will and because she was able to place the bruise in a manageable perspective.

A friend of mine practiced a variant on the kissing ritual for her daughter's bumps and bruises. When her little girl, Sarah, was hurt, she would get a kiss, then she would get a bandage on the spot where it hurt. Some days little Sarah would walk around with 15 or 20 bandages, which reminded her of her mother's magic healing.

By following some simple guidelines, you can imbue your kisses with more magical, painkilling power.

1. Kiss your babies a lot.

2. If your baby or toddler falls, gets hurt, or is feeling pain, make a special magic kissing ceremony.

3. Use this kind of kissing ceremony only for pain.

4. Use the same verbal expressions each time you perform a kissing ceremony (e.g., "Here, let me kiss that better"). Inject a bit of caring solemnity into the ceremony.

5. Follow the kissing with other comforting activities like hugs, rocking, and distraction. Keep that up until the pain has abated.

6. Act as if you believe in the benefit of your own kisses (even if you are a doubter). Avoid teasing your child about the pain. If it is a serious matter for him or her, stay with that mode until he or she is ready to lighten up. You need not force lightness with tickling or jokes unless your child is really ready.

Some children are born rationalists. As much as she likes the hugs and kisses for their own sake, my middle daughter (age six) has told me in no uncertain terms that kisses have no magical power. Nevertheless, I believe that kissing still eases her pain when she has it, and she gets a kiss despite her skepticism.

Cultivate a Soothing Tone of Voice

All children's ears are tuned to distinguish different tones of voice. Babies, who do not have language to decipher meaning, probably rely on it more heavily than older children. Try softly crooning a lullaby to your baby. It is a very pleasant experience for the singer as well as the baby. Paradoxically, when your baby needs your soothing croon the most, it may be at a time when you feel the least capable of producing such a sound. With a little practice and a lot of self-discipline, you can learn to lull yourself into a sufficiently soothing state of mind to calm even a colicky baby. Your voice is one of several tools you will need to use day after day to cope with the type of shrill, distressed cry that colicky babies produce. You will also need something called *presence of mind*—that is, an ability to stay rational even under intense strain. Presence of mind is what enables you to remember to give yourself five-minute breaks from a screaming baby in order to regain a sense of control and calm.

Taking Care of Yourself

Soothing Yourself (and Your Colicky Baby)

Colic affects parents by making them feel helpless, inadequate, often alone, and even angry and unsupported by friends and family who may lack credence in their plight.

Vignette: Colicky Fred Frazzles Frank and Carol

Frank and Carol thought of themselves as seasoned parents by the arrival of Fred, their third baby. The older two, Mark and Melinda, had had their share of sicknesses and crying spells. Frank and Carol prided themselves on rarely losing their cool with babies. Frank had always shared the middle-of-the-night awakenings for bottles or diapers with Carol. They were both looked to by their friends as a source of parenting tips because they always seemed so adept.

Baby Fred spent only one full night in the hospital after a quick delivery the previous evening. He had slept soundly between feedings, so there seemed to be no reason to stay a second night. The first week-and-a-half at home also went like a charm. Mark and Melinda were still excited about their new brother. Fred was not yet a threat to their privileged positions in the family. Frank and Carol were proud of having prepared themselves better for Fred's homecoming than they had for the first two.

Why Me?

Soon the honeymoon was over. Fred began to cry inconsolably for hours on end, starting at about three in the afternoon, and persisting almost nonstop into the wee hours of the next morning. Soon Mark and Melinda were complaining about the noise. At first, Frank and Carol hung in there, taking turns through the evening and night, resigning themselves to eating dinner standing up, with the wailing baby in one arm. After three days without a break, Carol's even temper was wearing thin. At least Frank could get away for nine hours a day and work in the relative peace of his office.

One afternoon, shortly before Frank returned from work, Fred awoke from his nap and immediately began to whimper. For the first time, Carol felt waves of rage welling up inside, which mystified and scared her. How could she feel this way toward a helpless infant, not yet a month old? Fred's wail crescendoed. Carol felt that if she didn't escape somewhere, she could end up hurting her baby. Tears welling up in her own eyes, she placed Fred, now roaring full blast, in his crib. She then walked into her bedroom, sat down on her bed, took a deep breath, cried a little, and dialed Fred's pediatrician.

Carol took Fred to Dr. Lopez, who had been Carol's family pediatrician since she was a little girl. Dr. Lopez

examined Fred. Then he asked Carol about the baby's eating, sleeping, and crying. In his own mind, Dr. Lopez satisfied himself that nothing serious was wrong with Fred. His
diagnosis was that Fred had colic and that Frank and Carol
would have to wait it out. He was not unsympathetic, but
having seen many a parent survive the ordeal, he saw little
reason to worry that Carol and Frank would be any different. He had confidence in them, and told her so, which had
helped in other situations. Now, however, confidence alone
was not going to do the trick. Carol needed assistance to
survive the next indeterminate number of weeks of emotional torture. She needed to do something for Fred to
soothe his distress, even if it was not effective all of the
time. She also needed to do something for herself; otherwise she would be unable to hang in there for her baby.

Don't Try to Cope Alone: Ask for and Accept Help

Carol deserves credit for admitting that she needed help
with Fred. Parents are led to think that if they can't handle
a crying baby, they should not have had a baby in the first
place. When you admit that you cannot cope with a very difficult child-care situation alone, you may be subjected to
unfair judgment by other parents who have never been in
your situation. Others might comment that Dr. Lopez said
Fred wasn't sick, so what's the big deal? Carol decided that
certain friends and family members were going to be sup-
portive of her and that certain others were just not able. She
was sad about this realization, for before Fred started crying, she had enjoyed the light-hearted friendship of some
mothers from the neighborhood.

Carol called her brother, sister, parents, three neighbors whose kids were teenage or older, and two baby-sitters from the local college baby-sitting service. She had her speech prepared: "Fred has colic and I need your help to get through the next several weeks. I can't do it alone. Can you give me two hours a week so I can get a rest and stay fresh?"

Carol was not just looking for a little extra rest. She understood that without the help she was asking for, she could not continue to give her children the mothering they needed—the patience, understanding, love, tenderness, and discipline that go out the window when one is under severe stress.

She worked up a calendar for the next four weeks, making sure that among family members, her husband, and paid babysitters, she had some break from Fred almost every day, even if it was for only an hour or two. Carol made sure that anyone who took care of Fred during his crying spells was prepared to follow her instructions on how to hold him and keep him as comfortable as possible. She showed them what kinds of motion and stimulation seemed to make things better or worse. And, very important, Carol extracted a promise that if Fred ever got to be too much to handle, they would say so immediately. After all, what would be the point of getting help if her helpers needed help?

Making Adjustments

Carol and Frank then sat down to discuss what else they could do to make things better for Fred, Mark, and Melinda. Frank suggested that for the time being, Mark should not have to share a bedroom with the baby. He was losing sleep and beginning to show resentment. Mark was pleased with this decision. Carol and Frank also remarked that they had stopped reading bedtime stories to the two older children and promised each other that they would not make Mark and Melinda pay for Fred's crying in that way.

Preserve Your Sanity

Next, they turned to the question of how to preserve their own sanity if only for Fred's sake. Frank said, "You know, Carol, I have to admit that when Fred is crying like he does, I get very tense and irritable. I wonder if Fred knows how tense I get." Both parents had learned some techniques of muscle relaxation and meditation in their prenatal classes. Carol suggested that they go back to practicing some of their relaxation techniques while they were carrying Fred around.

Carol had learned during labor with each of her three children that it was possible to be in excruciating pain and at the same time take steps to distance her mind from the intensity of the situation. She had also learned how to allow her body to relax and "go with the flow" rather than to fight against the labor contractions. By analogy, she and Frank could learn how to hold their screaming infant and, by singing a soothing melody, relax their own bodies and minds.

Carol called their old prenatal teacher, Eva, who, by virtue of her interest in nonmedical approaches to health, had several ideas for them. First, Eva gave them an audio-taped relaxation exercise to practice. They were to relearn how to go into a deep state of relaxation by practicing away from Fred at first. Then when they were proficient, they could practice keeping mind and body serene and could relax *despite* Fred's crying.

Mom's Diet

Then Eva suggested some dietary changes Carol might try, in case Fred's distress was in part related to a problem digesting some of the ingredients in Carol's breast milk. While there is little scientific proof of such a relationship, Carol was willing to consider the possibility. She had little to lose and much to gain. Eva explained to Carol that the best way to learn whether her diet was a contributor was to change only one food at a time, then allow enough time to see if elimination of a specific food from her diet led to less crying in subsequent feedings. Carol was systematic about removing roughage, wheat, and dairy from her diet over the ensuing weeks. While Fred's crying waxed and waned, it was never clear whether dietary changes were helping. Eva also suggested some herbal teas that, according to some folk traditions, render mother's milk a salve to colicky babies. One of the teas that contained some chamomile seemed to calm Carol down and make her feel more at ease. She continued to drink some every day just before Fred's crying was about to start. That helped her get into the right frame of mind to do her relaxation exercise while she held, diapered, breast-fed, and mothered her baby.

Magic: Apparent or Real?

A week after her call, Eva offered to drop by during one of Fred's evening "witching hours." As expected, when Eva arrived after dinner, Fred was in full gear, screaming with his back arched away from Frank, face red, his sister and brother hiding in the basement in front of the TV with the volume turned up in competition with Fred's decibels. Frank had Fred cradled in his left arm, and with beads of perspiration on his forehead, he was putting dishes away with his right arm. Carol was taking a one-hour break from the fracas. She had gone out in the car to get some peace and quiet and to refuel for the long evening ahead.

When Eva asked to hold Fred, Frank shrugged his shoulders and smiled weakly. "With pleasure," he said. Eva turned Fred around so that his face was away from hers, held him around his arching tummy with her large hands, and began to croon a melody that her grandfather had sung to her when she was a baby. Ten minutes later, when Carol came through the door, Eva was in the rocking chair and Fred was fast asleep in her arms. Frank told Carol how amazing it was to see Fred calm down like that. Carol felt thankful but confused and dismayed. Does this mean we are inadequate parents, she thought? What can Eva do that I can't do? Anticipating her reaction, Eva reassured her and Frank that they were the very best parents. The reason Fred stopped crying was that Eva offered a fresh approach, did not feel burnt out, and had the luck to catch Fred at a moment when he was ready for a nap.

Frank and Carol admitted to themselves that what they and Fred were going through was extraordinarily difficult. They asked for help and got it. They made adjustments in their daily routine to protect Fred's brother and sister. They took serious steps to take better care of themselves. Frank squeezed in a few minutes of exercise despite his exhaustion and changed his work schedule so he could be home earlier to help Carol. Carol meditated every day. They both practiced relaxation techniques when they were holding Fred during his crying spells. Carol drank chamomile tea and continued to be alert for any sign of a relationship between her diet and Fred's distress. She also learned some of Eva's songs and watched closely how she held Fred to induce him to sleep. It was difficult at first to accept that somebody outside the family could key into Fred's needs, but as soon as Carol saw that Eva could remain peaceful and serene in the most tense of situations, she was ready to learn from her.

Fred's Colic Begins to Improve

After a few weeks of coping and learning, Fred's screaming bouts began to gradually abate. Fred still cried for long stretches every day but there were breaks, and his sleep began to improve. Carol was still concerned about Fred. His pain was obvious to her. She wanted to do more for Fred than to merely relax herself, although she now saw the value in that. She looked into herbal and over-the-counter remedies for babies with colic. Dr. Lopez gave her a preparation to reduce gas in Fred's stomach, offering no guarantees that it would help. Frank and Carol enjoyed learning how to do a special baby massage and were surprised when it made Fred coo with delight. They began to understand that giving Fred as many pleasurable experiences as they could was an important antidote to his pain.

By the time Fred was 15 weeks old, he was much better. He still had irritable moments, especially during the "witching hour" in the evening, but his crying now fell within the bounds of what most parents would call "normal" for a baby of his age and temperament. If asked, Frank and Carol would never want to go through this kind of ordeal again if they could avoid it. However, they both felt that they matured as parents. They understood a valuable secret to coping with highly distressing situations: change what you can and learn to adjust to what cannot be changed. Fred felt his parents' confidence and peace of mind, and directly benefited from that.

Distraction

You can distract your child's attention by filling his or her consciousness with an activity or sensory experience that is interesting, engaging, and absorbing. Section II explained how the pain a five-year-old experiences from getting her finger caught in a door travels from her finger, to her spinal column, and to her brain. She reflexively pulls her finger away before additional damage is done. By definition, her reflexes work without her conscious awareness. Her eye blinks, whether she asks it to or not, when a foreign object comes near it. Only with a high degree of self-control can she override a reflex. So why, you may ask, did nature give us pain sensations if we don't need them to pull away from danger? Why aren't we constructed in such a way that our reflexes spare us the indignity and nuisance of feeling pain? One reason is that the damaged finger will still need attention after the fact. If the girl is watching as the door closes on her finger, she might begin to feel the pain before the damage is done. If not, she may not notice it until a few seconds have passed. Some observers mistakenly take this delay to indicate that her pain is exaggerated. This is not at all true. Rather, it is a good example of the power of distraction to temporarily escape even from intense pain.

Understanding a bit about attention and concentration can help you learn how to distract your child's attention from pain sensations. From early infancy, we are able to focus in on one activity, pretty much to the exclusion of others. To a baby at the breast, his mouth sensations are in the foreground of his awareness. Other feelings and sensations are available to awareness but at various distances in the background.

To a nine-year-old running up a soccer field toward a game-winning goal, his awareness of the game is in the foreground, while any aches and pains he might have incurred during the game up until then recede far into the background. He may be so wrapped up in the game that he will be surprised when you announce that the time clock has run out, and he has been playing for a whole hour. And he might be shocked when, upon taking his shin pads and socks off, he finds a few black and blue bruises on his ankles.

Once he does see them, only then might he begin to notice the aching pain from the bruises. This phenomenon is called *dissociation*. We dissociate or split our awareness between two different activities or feelings. Children's ability to dissociate can help them cope with painful situations. When you attempt to distract your child, you concoct an activity for him or her in order to help split his or her awareness between pain sensations and activities that you devise for distraction. The pain sensations and the activity compete for the child's attention. The child is given a mental option to tune in or out to either the pain or the activity or both.

Distraction is an effective tool for controlling pain when you have some warning before it occurs, as with a dental procedure, an immunization, removal of sutures, or, on a less serious note, brushing tangled hair, cutting finger- and toenails, or receiving a bump or bruise during playful roughhousing. The key to effective distraction is finding some activity or stimulation that completely absorbs your child's attention. The more deeply absorbed the child is, the more effectively distracted he or she will be.

Sucking Absorbs Baby's Attention

For very small babies, as previously illustrated, sucking is a potent distraction. Many physicians suggest timing painful

procedures such as immunizations, blood tests, even circumcision so that they are closely followed by breast- or
bottle-feeding or by sucking on a pacifier. Remember that
sucking is not only for distraction! It is also for nutrition
and for comfort that goes with nurturing. If your baby is
about to go through a painful medical procedure, has fallen
and bumped his or her head, or is irritated for no apparent
reason, you may want to give sucking its best chance of success by creating a setting most conducive to absorbing the
baby's attention. This could include:

- going to a quiet room if you have one

- deciding not to take phone calls for the next half hour

- relaxing your own body and mind

- speaking and singing in a soothing voice

- rocking gently in a chair

- concentrating on the baby's response to your voice
  and body motion

Novel Sights and Sounds Catch and Absorb Toddlers' Attention

Toddlers and preschoolers can be distracted for brief periods by visually interesting stimuli, such as a funny cartoon
or even a person in a cartoon character suit. Be careful, however, not to present a child with a figure that he or she is
afraid of. Many toddlers are afraid of clown faces, cartoon
characters, and strangers. For children age two and up, distraction is most effective if it is implemented before a
painful event begins. A pediatric dentist allowed my tod-

dler to pick a favorite cartoon to put in the VCR while he began to examine his teeth. Only when he was very involved with the cartoon did the dentist attempt to poke and prod inside my son's mouth. All the while he explained to my son what he was doing.

Distraction Is a Dual Awareness

Distraction takes advantage of *split* awareness, which is not the same as substituting one awareness for another. From my child's perspective, he was into the cartoon and knew full well that the dentist was peering into his mouth, talking about what he was doing. At any time, my son could have chosen to focus his attention in one place or the other, or both. This dual focus puts the child in the driver's seat as far as how much discomfort he wants and needs to attend to. At no time should distraction be used to trick a child into cooperating with a painful or frightening procedure.

In fact, I tell a child before a shot, for example, that the shot will hurt a bit, but that it might bother him less if he is involved in a video game or some other play activity. Why this works has to do with your authority and your child's trust and confidence in your role as benevolent protector. Paradoxically, just as you are about to "betray" your children by allowing them to experience pain (even if for a good reason), you are using your parental power to convince your children that they can be less afraid *if* they do just as you say. Therefore you must have confidence in your own authority and "magical protective power" for your suggestions to work. This will be illustrated further in the section on hypnosis.

By Age Eight, Many Kids Can Distract Themselves

By the second grade, most children have developed some knowledge about their own attention span. To function in class effectively, they have learned to shift focus back and forth between the teacher and their desk work. Most classes have a significant amount of ambient noise, and most children can effectively tune that out to concentrate on difficult mental tasks. Using these very same abilities, children eight years old and up can learn to distract themselves without adult prompting. Once a boy or girl has been taught or has stumbled on a way of focusing the mind on something other than a painful sensation or experience, that way or method can be used repeatedly, as long as there is not too much anxiety.

Biting the Bullet (Squeezing the Hand)

One way kids learn to distract themselves is to create their own competing sensations. The expression "bite the bullet" comes from a wartime practice before the days of anesthesia when wounded soldiers controlled their pain during medical treatment by biting down hard on something like a bullet. The soldiers were inducing a controlled sensation of pain in the teeth and jaw to compete with the pain coming from the wound. The virtue of this type of distraction is that the person controls his own pain by controlling its competing sensation. The more in control one feels, the less anxious one becomes. The more intense the controlled sensation, the more effective it will be at competing for conscious awareness. Inasmuch as it is unhealthy to put bullets between your child's teeth, there are many analogous ways to bite the bullet. Boys and girls as young as four years of age can be convinced to squeeze very tightly onto an adult's hand during a painful procedure. If blood needs to be drawn from one forearm, the child can squeeze an adult's hand with her opposite hand. Tell the child that the harder she squeezes, the more she will feel the squeezed fist, and the less she will be bothered by the other arm. She may not believe you, but that's OK as long as she is willing to try the technique. Independent-minded children are more likely to squeeze their fists without holding onto yours.

Creating a Pain Dial

An eight-year-old had to have a dental appliance adjusted once a day by inserting a crank into the appliance and rotating it one half turn, causing pain in his upper jaw and face. Each evening before it was time to adjust the appliance, he would take an acetaminophen per his orthodontist's instructions. Then he would find a tennis ball, lie back on his bed, and tell his father or mother when he was ready. The first time he used the squeeze method, he was dubious and became disappointed that squeezing the ball failed to eliminate all discomfort. The boy felt discouraged from trying the same method again if it was not going to live up to his initial expectations. His father clarified that squeezing the ball was not going to eliminate the pain in his jaw. What it would do is help him pay less attention to it. The next evening his father suggested that he squeeze the ball harder when the pain was worse and softer when the pain was less severe. He tried this on several subsequent days, and soon he would not sit for the cranking unless he had his tennis ball in hand. When asked, the boy readily acknowledged that the more he thought his dental appliance would hurt when it was being adjusted, the harder he would have to squeeze a tennis ball in his hand. For him, the technique became more than just distraction. He turned his fist into a "pain dial" that he could turn up or down at will by adjusting his grip. Now he moved from control over his jaw pain to mastery over the fear and pain. He knew it would still hurt every time, but he was no longer afraid or anxious.

What is special about squeezing a tennis ball that enables a child to regulate his discomfort level? Some kinds of distraction are predominantly sensory. Having a child watch a video, a clown, or a cuckoo clock, or having him listen to interesting music requires very little effort on the part of the child. Squeezing the fist or a ball, on the other hand, requires premeditated motor action. By deciding to squeeze the ball, then squeezing it hard, the child is actively creating the distracting sensation in his own hand and arm, and ultimately in the area in his brain where he experiences pain.

Coach Your Child to Breathe for Distraction

In many respects, squeezing the ball accomplishes similar results to Lamaze breathing for childbirth. Children can be taught to breathe in a way to create vivid sensations in their diaphragm, chest, and stomach that is sufficient to compete with other painful sensations. This kind of breathing is not necessarily meant to be strictly relaxing, although it can have that effect. Women are taught to adjust the intensity of their Lamaze breathing to match the intensity of labor. The breathing carries the added benefit of assuring a good oxygen supply to mother and child through the ordeal. Likewise, children need to be coached in breathing techniques so they do not make themselves dizzy by hyperventilating.

Before you take your child to a medical visit requiring cavity fillings, immunizations, removal of stitches, or any other uncomfortable procedure, demonstrate for the child the pace and type of breathing that would be desirable to maintain. Then practice this during a mock procedure. You may want to count out loud to pace the child's respiration, or, if she can see your face, have her follow your rate of breathing with her own. Practice paying attention to the physical sensations that go with the breathing. Have the child focus on the feelings in her stomach, diaphragm, mouth, and lips as she inhales and exhales. Then during the actual procedure, remind her that the breathing does not eliminate the pain—rather, it gives her more control over it. Afterward, ask her how much the procedure hurt. Then ask how much control she felt she had over the discomfort. She may say truthfully that it hurt just the same as always but that she felt less nervous and more in charge.

Help Your Child Distract Himself from Recurrent Pain

One of the reasons that untreated chronic pain can do insidious emotional damage is that it makes you feel trapped. After some time it feels like there is no beginning and no end to the pain. It becomes a part of being. This kind of thinking is difficult to distinguish from depression. Distraction can be an effective remedy, especially when the distraction is initiated and conceived by the child him- or herself. Once again, the goal of distracting oneself from chronic or recurrent pain is modest and limited. A child will not buy the idea that "getting busy" will alleviate his chronic recurrent headaches. If you suggest that he watch TV or read a book to take his mind off the pain, he is likely to react angrily. He might think you are implying that the pain is so easy to ignore that he could simply will it away. The more realistic approach is to suggest that when he gets himself busy, absorbing his own attention in something that interests him, he might experience the pain as less in the mental foreground and more in the background. He needs to be reassured that you are not minimizing his discomfort and that you know that mere distraction does not make pain disappear. You might suggest that he capitalize on something he probably does all the time on his own without being aware of it. For example, you could point out a recent activity that so engaged his attention that, though he still felt the pain, it did not bother or worry him as much.

As you might gather, it is not always easy to convince a child that he or she is capable of taking back some control. But it is worth the effort! The reason to take back control is not to make the pain go away, but rather to regain the feeling of being in control of the senses, the ability to attend and concentrate, and to participate in life. The alternative can be a growing feeling of helplessness and hopelessness—even depression. When you appeal to a child on the level of control rather than on the pain itself, he or she is more likely to feel understood. When a child feels understood, it is much easier for him or her to take your advice. Often, after all is said and done, children will attest to the benefit of using distraction. They may even exaggerate, boasting to their friends about how "easily" they made it through a painful or frightening procedure, or a period of suffering from headache or stomachache. This is a good kind of pride, borne of mastery over fear.

Relaxation

A child who can learn to let go of muscle tension for a specific purpose like counteracting pain or anxiety has a very special gift. It means that he or she can be an active participant in whatever it will take to heal a source of pain. You do not need to make sure the child is in a relaxed state of mind for distraction to be fully effective. You can easily distract your child's attention when he or she is fully alert and energetic. It might be obvious why children do better at controlling pain and fear with distraction and why adults do better with relaxation. Most children do not like to sit still, especially when they are afraid or uncomfortable. Perhaps adults can master the ability to sit still and confine their jitters to the mind. Nevertheless, there are many situations where it is very helpful to teach your child some relaxation techniques to counteract pain, anxiety, or even simple muscle tension.

When adults want to relax, many of us know how to lie back on a comfortable chair, allow our respiration to slow down, take a few deep breaths, make a big stretch with arms and legs extended as when you wake up in the morning, and then voluntarily relax the muscles of the body. The best way to get children to become physically and mentally relaxed is through use of imagination and fantasy. Think of your willful four- or five-year-old who says she has a tummyache and prefers to stay home from nursery school one day. You know that asking her to "make her muscles let go of their tension" will at best be lost on her and, at worst, induce her to a higher state of tension.

Instead, find an imaginary image or metaphor that she might find intriguing, and incorporate the image into a game. You might suggest, for example, playing a game where you take turns pretending you are like different animals that evoke a sense of peacefulness. "I'll be a bird, gliding on the wind, and you'll be a sea otter, basking in the sun." You can go further and try suggesting things like "your legs and arms are like branches of a tree near a garden, blowing in a gentle warm breeze, and your body is the trunk, stretching toward the sky. And I'll be the breeze. . . ."

It can be enjoyable to use your own creativity to invent ideas and images that draw your child into a feeling of calm and relaxation. This kind of play is a way of subtly conveying the fact that your child can learn to exert control over his or her own bodily reactions. Once you do this a few times, your child can learn to use the idea of "mind over matter" by him- or herself. This "knowledge" is intuitive, not scientific. Children as young as five or six can come to appreciate the power of their own imagination over their body's physical state. When you join in with creating and acting out the playful images, you are setting an example or model for your child to emulate as well. If you do it, and you appear to be reaping the same pleasures and benefits that you are trying to convey to your child, it will seem more attractive, more real, more doable to your child.

Breathing for Relaxation

Breath control, diaphragmatic breathing, belly breathing, and deep breathing are just a few of the expressions used to describe various relaxation techniques. Earlier paragraphs described the role of breathing as a form of mental distraction. Young children often lack the patience and concentration needed to learn the sustained kind of breath control that is sometimes needed to achieve a state of deep relaxation. Some children, however, are temperamentally suited for this.

Children who suffer from frequent bouts of stomachaches, headaches, muscle pain, and physical problems that get in the way of daily functioning may gain a great deal from practicing a breathing technique several times a day. Children who seem to lack patience and attention can start by spending as little as two or three minutes at a time, and very gradually working up to as long as 20- or 30-minute stretches of uninterrupted breathing for relaxation.

The best way to teach your child is to teach yourself at the same time. Sit in an upright position with your child beside you, near you, or even in your lap in a comfortable chair. Have your child put his or her hands on the stomach and feel it move up and down with each breath. Following is an example of what you can say to teach this technique to your child.

> "Let's have a few minutes of peaceful quiet together. Breathe slowly with me like this: in two, three, out, two, three, four. Now let's close our eyes and breathe slowly and steadily together. In, out, in, out," etc. Then say, "Imagine that each time you breathe out, you feel a bit more comfortable, relaxed, and peaceful. Every breath lets some more tension and pain out. Every breath lets some fresh energy in."

Continue this for a few minutes the first time, stopping when your child becomes fidgety or uncomfortable. You do not necessarily need to mention that these sessions are expressly for controlling pain. Their general purpose is to teach the child to slow down his or her own overall level of physical and emotional arousal. Once the child is able to do this, he or she can apply this skill to any number of situations, including times of pain, fear, distress, or anxiety. Pick a regular time of day to practice the relaxation technique. The more you do it, the more natural it feels. You will also find that it gets easier to concentrate on the breath and keep your mind free of distractions after a week or so of daily practice. The best time to practice is before a meal when you are not drowsy. Many adults and children fall asleep when practicing in a state of fatigue or close to bedtime.

Progressive Muscle Relaxation

Children live in their bodies and experience the world physically and kinesthetically in addition to the way we as adults do, which is through sight, sound, and thought. The basic idea behind muscle relaxation is that tense muscles arise from pain, distress, anxiety, and overall nervousness. Even though the tense muscles may not arise out of a particular injury, they can compound and complicate existing problems. Conversely, the more you can relax your muscles, the more you calm the parts of the body that are not sick, injured, or inflamed. By sharing your ability to voluntarily relax your muscles with your child, you provide yet another way of exerting a feeling of self-control over a body that sometimes acts as if it has a mind of its own. Progressive muscle relaxation is well suited to older children and teenagers who need a structured way to mentally and physically warm up for intense physical or mental activities, but who, due to exuberance and impatience, risk injury by diving right in. Teens also have the body control and the attention span to use this on their own. With an adult's verbal coaching and guidance, younger children (ages five and up) can also use this technique.

How and When to Relax the Muscles

Have the child lie on his or her back on the floor or in a reclining chair. Begin with a big full-body stretch as when you awake in the morning. Next, have the child take a deep breath in and slowly let it out, closing the eyes. Then the coach or guide can lead the meditation with the following.

> "Now just imagine that your body is as light as a feather, floating on a bed of air, an inch above the ground. With every breath, your body can become just a bit more and more relaxed. Now concentrate on your left and right hands. On the count of three, make a tight fist with both hands and hold that fist tightly while I count to five: one, two, three, four, five. Now let go of the fist and let both hands go from being very tense and tight to very relaxed. Remember the contrast between tense and relaxed as you imagine that the tension floats up and out of your hands and arms into the air. Next, turn your attention to your feet and ankles. When I count to three, tense your feet by curling your toes up toward your knees as far as you can, holding it until I reach five, and let go, again remembering the contrast between the feeling of tense and relaxed."

Continue telling the child to tense and relax his or her upper leg muscles by squeezing the knees together and releasing; tense the stomach by pulling the belly in (without holding the breath) and letting go; tense the shoulders and neck by shrugging the shoulders up to the ears, and letting them drop down; tense the mouth by pursing the lips tightly together and releasing them; tense the forehead by raising the eyebrows up to the sky and letting them down; and finally the eyes, by shutting them tightly (but not too tightly) and releasing. I always encourage children to enjoy that feeling of being relaxed and comfortable, and to remember the feeling well so that in the future they can let their muscles relax whenever they want to.

A good time to practice progressive muscle relaxation is before or after intense physical or mental activity, as a type of warm-up or cooldown for the body and the mind. It is an excellent practice for physical-education teachers or sports coaches who wish to foster a positive attitude in children about their own bodies. Competitively athletic children need a great deal of encouragement and reminding to take these measures to lower the risk of injury.

I have also encouraged a number of high school students to practice a relaxation technique before taking a major examination, often with good results. Going into a complex mental task in a relaxed state of body and mind facilitates clear thinking and a feeling of being "in the zone" of optimum performance.

Helpful Hints to Avoid Frustration

Soothing instrumental music can be useful to help your child get into and stay in the mood to practice relaxation techniques. Nature's own music—birds, water, cicadas, or the rainfall on the roof—can do the trick nicely. If you use the same background sounds each time you practice relaxation, the sounds themselves will become associated with the feeling in your child's mind. When that happens, the sounds will be helpful by themselves in evoking the right mood and feeling of relaxation. Many of my patients have learned to become very relaxed on hearing the sound of my audiotaped voice giving relaxation instructions.

A couple of tips: you do not need absolute quiet to relax. To the contrary, like a baby learning to sleep, it's better to get used to a moderate amount of ambient noise than to rely on utter silence to concentrate or relax. Make it a point not to answer the telephone while you are practicing. Ask others in the house to take care of that or the doorbell until you are done. Do not be concerned if you or the child should become easily distracted by sights, sounds, or even thoughts while you are learning how to relax. The goal is not to be free from distraction. Rather, it is to not be bothered by extraneous thoughts and feelings. Have faith that after several practice sessions, distractions become less bothersome.

Some children take to relaxation training like ducks to water. For others, the benefit rolls like water off a duck's back. The youngest child with whom I have had success with relaxation techniques was a five-year-old girl. Preteens and teenagers are most able to use relaxation if they wish. I have watched a number of children between the ages of 10 and 17 who were able to place themselves into such a deep state of reverie that they learned to endure multiple painful, invasive medical procedures in the hospital. They behave similarly to the way patients do when under the influence of morphine—aware of the pain, but somehow less bothered by it. Children who are not temperamentally well suited to deep relaxation respond better to various forms of mental and physical distraction.

One fact that is known by pain specialists, but not understood by the general public, is that people respond in their own individual ways to efforts at pain control. Give 10 people with the same type of tension headache the same dose of aspirin, and they will all respond differently. Some will get immediate relief, others delayed relief. Some people's ability to take antipain medications are so hampered by unwanted side effects that they are unwilling or unable to tolerate a therapeutic dosage and thereby cannot get relief.

Others, in contrast, seem unfazed by most any pain medication. The same thing goes for breathing, distraction, and relaxation. Some children appear to become even more upset and agitated when they try to relax. It is as if they cannot let their guard down lest upsetting thoughts and feelings flood in. Fortunately, such children are part of a fairly small minority.

When you want to combine relaxation, breathing, and distraction into one technique to coach your child through a period of pain, discomfort, or distress, you can employ a type of fantasy called imaginative involvement.

Using Imagination and Fantasy

Guided Imagery: Painting a Picture in Your Child's Mind's Eye

Guided imagery can be used to transform the child's feelings of discomfort into feelings that are more tolerable and less frightening. Guided imagery is a way of telling a story embellished with pleasant sensory, emotional, and cognitive images and content. In other words, you paint a pleasant picture in your child's mind's eye. It is most effective when the child hearing the story is in a state of physical relaxation, although this is not required. The goal is to capture the child's attention with a plausible brief story or vignette that incorporates vivid pleasant sensations within its text. Following is an example:

> Close your eyes. Imagine that you are walking alone on a warm summer morning on a deserted ocean shore. Bend over and take off your shoes. Feel the texture of the sand as it pushes up between your toes, as you walk slowly toward the breaking waves. As you walk, feel the ripples on the sand created by the wind of the night before. Feel the warm sun gently caressing your shoulders, the light, salty breeze that you can taste and smell as it ruffles your hair. Listen to the rhythmic sound of the waves breaking against the shore about 50 yards away, and the seagulls' laughing calls as they circle playfully overhead. If you listen more closely, you notice the rushing of the breeze through some leaves in the distant stand of trees several hundred yards away. Now keep walking very slowly toward the breaking waves and see the glint of the morning sun against the rippling ocean, a sailboat drifting at anchor in the distance, and the white salt spray as the waves crash against the shiny, wet sand at the shoreline. Sit down on the soft sand, just at the spot before the sand gets wet. Move your hands

through the sand, and feel the fine grains trickle
through the fingers of both your hands. As a large
wave crashes, feel a fine mist of salty air blow
across your face. Taste the salt spray. Take it in
with your nostrils. Try to do more than just
imagine being there. *Be* there at the beach. Take
in the experience with all of your senses. Stay
there for a while. Go there every once in a while
when you need a break from your (painful
condition). It is your place. A place where you can
feel refreshed, healthy, relaxed, and free from the
worries of the day.

Each child and adult can usually think of a scene like
this—a place and time where there are no worries, aches,
pain, or discomfort. The best way to tap into the reservoir
of a child's imagination is to have him or her help you select
one or two places like this. Many children cannot think of
an ideal place and need a little prompting and coaching.
Some are afraid of water, mountains, woods, and nature
and find solace and peace when they imagine sitting in front
of the TV at home. Guided imagery works best if the scene
you evoke for the child is easy to imagine, clear, vivid, and
rich with sensory information. The richer the scene, the
easier it is for the child to call it up in his or her imagination, and the more effective it will be in temporarily blocking out awareness of unpleasant sensations, thoughts, or
feelings.

You can invent a 15- to 20-minute vignette incorporat-
ing the relaxing pleasant image into a simple narrative, like
a walk to the beach, a picnic at the park, an afternoon at
home with Grandma cooking dinner, or a swim in the river.
Then construct the vignette with the child's help and elim-

inate aspects of the story that work poorly. Practice with the child once or twice a day "going to that pleasant place," for a week or so. At that time, the child can go there without adult supervision. Sometimes it helps to make an audiotape of the vignette so the child can listen to it when you are unavailable. Include instructions on deep breathing and relaxation before introducing the guided image on the tape. A relaxed child can attend to the content of the tape more easily. Then the boy or girl can take the tape to school, camp, or the doctor's office if ever needed to control emotional distress or physical pain.

Guided imagery is not a substitute for talking about problems, and we are not advocating a form of escapism. Rather it is a tool for gaining a sense of control over episodes of pain or distress. While guided images do not have a direct effect on pain itself, they are a potent way to ease anxiety and distress. As noted many times in this book, a more anxious child feels pain more acutely, is more bothered by physical discomfort, and is more easily agitated and irritated. By use of guided imagery, you can effectively lower his tension level and raise his pain threshold, helping him to cope better with sources of pain and stress.

Imaginative Involvement

Once you are familiar with teaching your children to relax, you are ready to combine all of the relaxation techniques into an interesting method of distraction and absorption called imaginative involvement. This method was developed by hospital child-care workers, nurses, and child psychologists who care for children undergoing painful, invasive, or frightening medical procedures in hospitals

or medical clinics. Some of the situations you might
encounter in everyday life that would benefit from imaginative involvement might include immunizations or drawing of blood samples, x-rays, dental and orthodontic
procedures, removal of nondissolving sutures, or removal of
splinters. Imaginative involvement can also be used to help
a child weather a particularly difficult headache or stomach
cramp, one in which the intensity of pain waxes and wanes.
You can also employ the technique to help children visual-
ize the effect of pain medications while waiting for them
to take effect.

What is imaginative involvement? When you draw your
child into a fantasy story, you are often able to deeply absorb
his or her attention to the sights, sounds, sensations, and
feelings felt by the characters in the story. You invent a fantasy story in which your child *is* the main character. You tell
the story so that the child's pain is incorporated into the
story, but incorporated in such a way that the pain is transformed into a more tolerable and familiar sensation with a
less frightening meaning.

For example, an 11-year-old girl, Lisa, loves gymnastics
but is terrified about a routine blood test. She can endure
self-induced pain and discomfort when practicing on the
uneven parallel bars. The difference between the two types
of pain is that one is under her control, and the other feels
as if it is beyond her control.

A day or two before the blood test, Lisa and her father
create a story in which she has made the national finals in
gymnastics. Lisa and her dad take turns developing and
embellishing the story so that it can be told and retold in
vivid detail, paying special attention to the physical sensations she would feel in her muscles, lungs, and hands while
performing a difficult routine.

To help her focus and concentrate on the story, Lisa sits in a comfortable chair and practices breathing and muscle relaxation techniques. After becoming deeply relaxed, Lisa and her father begin to tell the story. They recount the vaults and the floor exercise, saving the uneven bars for last. Lisa absorbs herself in the thoughts, feelings, and sensations of swinging, letting go, tumbling through the air, grabbing again, and feeling the enormous forces of gravity challenging her aerial acrobatics. Lisa and her father then select a particularly intense, exciting moment in the routine during which she can easily imagine her muscles being pushed to the limit of her strength and endurance. At that moment during each retelling of the story, Lisa weaves the feeling of an intravenous needle poking through her arm into the flood of sensations. "As I fly backward from the upper to the lower bar, the needle is in place. Then, as my two hands slap against the lower bar and grab with all my might, the needle goes in. I swing round into a back flip with a full twist, and nail a perfect dismount as the needle enters the vein."

Lisa and her dad rehearse this imaginative story on the day before the procedure, adding in one additional element. At the same moment Lisa imagines the needle enter her skin, she can squeeze her dad's wrist (as if it were a parallel bar), and her dad can press his finger or the back of a pencil against the spot where she will receive the injection. In this way, Lisa practices dual awareness. She simultaneously feels the excitement of the vigorous gymnastic routine and the sharp sting of the IV needle. There is no need to "distract" Lisa's attention away from the pain of the needle. In this approach, Lisa incorporates the pain of the needle into the self-controlled, self-induced pain felt every time she does this particular maneuver. Once Lisa has practiced the story at home with her father, she is ready for the real thing.

It is a big help if the doctor and nurse are aware of Lisa's preparation and are willing to allow her to incorporate her imaginary story into the blood-drawing procedure. It is also good for the nurse or doctor to understand that they are not trying to sneak up on Lisa with the needle! In fact, even with the imaginative involvement going in full swing, many children want the doctor or nurse to count to three before inserting the needle, all the better to time the story to the procedure to get the best effect.

Some other examples of this technique can include the following. Have a child imagine getting knocked over by a big wave while playing in the surf at the beach, then weave that into a story that can be told while receiving dental drilling or an immunization. Or, imagine riding a bicycle down a bumpy road standing up on the pedals, legs and arms working like shock absorbers, while a splinter is being removed from the foot. A child with a headache and fever could imagine pumping his legs on a swing, propelling himself in higher and higher arcs, with a cool breeze blowing against his face. In the imagination, the child can be in as much control as he or she wishes over the intensity of the sensations.

For best results, imaginative involvement should be combined with relaxation and guided breathing. Make up the imaginary vignette with the child, taking turns telling it until you arrive at a version that will work well. Choose a moment in the vignette to incorporate the painful target sensation or procedure. Rehearse the story and at the same time simulate the painful procedure. Have the child incorporate some physical action into the imagined vignette, such as clenching the fists at the climactic moment. Tell the medical practitioner about your preparations and enlist his or her cooperation.

Hypnotic Suggestion

Hypnosis: How to Shift Your Child's Focus of Attention

The sample guided image of the beach described in detail earlier incorporates something called *hypnotic suggestion* at the very end. When you say, "You can feel safe, healthy, refreshed, and free from fear and distress when you visit this place," you are planting a plausible idea into the narrative in a relaxed, noncoercive way. The child has the choice to buy the suggestion or ignore it altogether. I think of it as suggesting another option for the child to redirect his or her thinking in a more positive way.

Hypnosis is a poorly understood method of pain control; however, various forms of hypnosis are used by health practitioners the world over. In a nutshell, hypnosis is a method of focusing attention and concentration on a particular line of thought and feeling to obtain a desired result. Hypnosis capitalizes on the widespread ability of most children to tune in to one line of thinking and at the same time tune out of conscious awareness other competing lines of thinking.

In a typical application of hypnotic technique, a child will attend to and concentrate on the sound of the hypnotist's voice. The voice (your voice) can gently direct the child to gradually relax his breathing, his muscles, and his whole body. With the child still listening to you, you can express your wishes, hopes, and positive belief in your child's ability to cope with his pain. These wishes and hopes should never be placed in the form of an imperative command, such as "you will relax." Children are quite able to hear your suggestions when they are couched in the language of free choice—"you may be more relaxed" or, "you can begin to feel stronger with every day."

You can use hypnotic suggestion with your child to encourage specific ways of coping, such as taking good care of his body, eating well, getting proper exercise, and seeing a doctor as needed. You can also suggest that the child focus his attention intently on a part of the body that is free of pain or discomfort. In one session with a child with a sore knee, I had her concentrate on her healthy strong heart, lungs, and circulation. Then she imagined that the painful throbbing sensations in her knee were also her circulation sending healing messages to the damaged area. The idea transformed her pain from something painful and scary into something hopeful. The knee still throbbed, but the girl was not so preoccupied with what the throbbing meant or whether it would ever stop.

Hypnosis is usually practiced by trained mental health practitioners and licensed hypnotists. Popular culture, movies, and nightclub hypnotists incorrectly portray hypnosis as a form of involuntary mind control by one person imposing his or her "powers" over another. For this reason, many parents are distrustful of health professionals working this way with their children. They fear that hypnosis could be used to put the child in a trance against his will or make the child do something against his own better judgment. When the idea of hypnosis is introduced as a simple method of refocusing attention in helpful ways, parents are generally more receptive to allowing its use.

For severe, intractable, and chronic pain problems it is advisable to seek the help of trained professionals. However, there are many ways that parents and caregivers make use of children's natural inborn ability to focus and refocus their attention at will. When you put your child in front of the TV, knowing that it will give you time to make a phone call, you understand that the TV captures his or her attention so intensely that your child is oblivious to your conversation. When your child is home from school with fever and headache from the flu, and you say, "If you sit on the couch and watch your favorite movie on the VCR, your head might feel a bit less achy," you are building on the distracting power of the VCR by using a form of hypnotic suggestion. Similarly, when you ceremoniously say, "Let me kiss your boo-boo and make it better," you are suggesting to your child that he or she can tap into a natural ability to alter the way he or she feels. As amazing as this may seem, there is nothing magical about it. The key phrases are "let me," indicating the child's choice to let you or not, and "better," acknowledging the fact that a kiss can *only* make it better, not make it go away.

Hypnosis works best to control children's pain when you alter the meaning of the pain from something frightening to something more positive, but still plausible. Thus, a finger stick in the doctor's office can be renamed a "pinch" without denying that it does hurt. A stomachache from overeating can be reframed as the body working very hard to digest a lot of food. A headache from a cold or the flu can be transformed into a reminder by the head that the child needs extra rest and sleep. When you say with the confident assurance of a parent, "If you do this, you will feel better," you are making use of hypnotic principles. A key to effective suggestion is to be unafraid of exuding that parental confidence to your child, even when you are not absolutely sure. If the pain does not go away, you will be forgiven, and you can try something else!

Preparing for Painful Procedures

The chapter on preparing for a visit to Dr. Driscoll, the dentist, illustrated an example of rehearsal as a way of helping the child feel ready for a scary, uncomfortable procedure. Now, having reviewed in greater detail some of the coping methods you can apply when preparing your child, we will return to this topic for added detail.

Many parents hesitate to prepare their children for a visit to the doctor or dentist for fear that it will just make them worried and uncooperative. One difficulty for the unprepared child is that it could undermine his trust in you or his doctor. He may never be sure whether a visit will entail something relatively benign like a tooth cleaning; a physical exam with weight, height, and blood pressure checks; or an invasive procedure like having a cavity filled, blood drawn, or stitches removed. If children had to go to the doctor or dentist only once in their whole life, it would probably not be essential to prepare them. But each time you do provide preparation and create realistic expectations, you build both trust and confidence for future visits, whether planned or unplanned.

Why Prepare Your Child?

Preparation for an invasive procedure gives a child a chance to gain a small piece of control over a situation in which she has little choice. She cannot choose to forgo medical or dental care. You as her caregiver must insist that she cooperate with something that she would not otherwise do on her own, something painful and frightening. By offering her a sense of control over some small part of what she is to experience, you give her an opportunity to face her own pain.

How to Prepare Your Child

Education. Education means communicating with your child so that he or she understands what is going to happen and why. Preparation gives you a chance to convey to a child what will be expected of her in any given situation. For a throat culture at the pediatrician's office, a six-year-old girl would like to be reassured that she is not going to have a shot! She would like to know what a throat culture is, how it is done, what will be asked of her, and what will not be asked of her. Many, but not all six-year-old girls would like to know *why* they need a throat culture as well. Experience tells us that a child who asks intelligent questions like this is going to learn coping skills much more quickly than a child who is not properly oriented to the circumstances.

Rehearsal. The second part of preparation is rehearsal of the procedure to be done by the doctor, dentist, nurse, or even barber if that presents a problem for your child. The purpose of playacting the procedure ahead of time is to familiarize you and your child with the setting, the players, the expectations, the duration, and the specifics of how the child must cooperate.

Thus, you can play out a visit to the barber with your rambunctious four-year-old. You can give him an idea of how to sit in the waiting area, look at magazines, watch other people get their hair cut first, and notice that they are not crying. You can show the child what kind of scissors the barber uses. You might explain that it does not hurt to cut hair, but that sometimes combing can catch snags that hurt a bit for a second. You can even practice the idea of getting a ride on the barber chair to inject some fun into the rehearsal. A visit to the barber shop on a different day than the cut itself is an excellent way to prepare a skittish child. It will stimulate questions and help you anticipate some of his concerns.

How long before a doctor visit should rehearsal begin?

Anyone who has ever rehearsed a part for a play knows that "opening night" is the focal point of the preparation. Likewise, you and your child rehearse for a medical procedure with full knowledge of when that procedure will happen. While you do not want your child to worry excessively for too long before a dental or medical appointment, informing him a day or two before enables you to "put the worry to work." Children who need to feel in control of their surroundings do better with more preparation, while other children are more able to "go with the flow."

Age two: Even a two-year-old benefits from being mentally prepared for the fact that he or she will be undergoing something uncomfortable. In the hours leading up to the visit, or even the night before, you can take the opportunity to explain that you will hold him in your lap and be there the whole time. By talking about it in simple language, you are providing a working vocabulary for your toddler to understand his unpredictable world.

Age three: Children under age three have at best a vague sense of what "tomorrow" means. For them, I suggest talking about a doctor visit the night before, around bedtime, but only in general terms, saving the specifics for the few hours leading up to the visit. At that time you can rehearse coping behaviors like squeezing your hand, getting hugs and kisses, and asking good questions of the doctor.

Ages four to five: Begin preparing 24 to 48 hours before. Preschoolers have irrational but understandable fears of shots and other medical invasions. Will the hole plug itself up after the shot? What is the bandage for? Preparation will arouse some of these worries before it is too late to do anything about them. You can show your four-year-old a scratch on someone's body that is healing or has already healed. You can go to the store and select a favorite theme-decorated bandage. Then you can rehearse the procedure a few times, taking turns playing the different roles. Letting the child be the doctor is a good way of eliciting more questions and concerns. Many boys and girls this age prefer to rehearse with a doll or action figure. It helps to have a toy doctor kit around the house too.

Ages six to eight: Prepare up to four days before a procedure. Children this age are still unafraid to show their fears and needs in scary situations, but they are knowledgeable enough to have concerns about their safety and inability to control themselves when frightened. A six-year-old can be told that a needle is sharp, and that if he is unable to hold still for a shot, he could get hurt.

He may respond by trying to talk you out of bringing him to the doctor altogether. You could interpret this as a test of your resolve and your ability to handle the worry. It is as if he is asking, "Can you make the visit feel safe enough for me? Are you going to be angry with me if I get too frightened?" At any age, your child needs you to be prepared to take charge of a frightening situation and set limits when and wherever necessary.

Ages nine and up: Ask your child how much preparation he or she would like before a dental or medical procedure. Some kids will ask not to be told until the day of an appointment, while others want to know right now about an appointment that is weeks away. You may not want to take your preadolescent's wishes too literally, but there is still value in responding to their stated need. You might discover that an older child wants more warning and preparation after all, especially if by preparing he or she develops some coping abilities.

Rehearsing coping skills. The third part of preparation is practicing coping skills during rehearsal. You can use your creativity to match a coping technique to the upcoming procedure and then practice that during the rehearsal. For example, when my son once prepared for an orthodontic visit, he selected a distracting technique (and acetaminophen) to help him cope with the discomfort of having his palate expander adjusted. He simulated the duration of the procedure by counting to 10. At the same time, he squeezed a tennis ball in his hand, paying close attention to the sensations it created in his arm. By rehearsing the procedure with the coping technique, my son gained confidence in his ability to control the intensity of the sensation in his hand, even as he would be aware of the pain in his upper jaw.

Because he would have to undergo the palate expander adjustment daily for a few weeks, he needed to know what kinds of things were under his control. Although he could not control how often to undergo the procedure, he could determine what time of day it was done. He could not control the fact that it was uncomfortable, but he could decide how hard to squeeze the tennis ball, or whether to take one or two Tylenol a half hour before.

Let us review some of the coping techniques you can suggest for and practice with your child to use in preparation for a painful procedure.

1. Remind the child of your presence and availability for emotional support.

2. Say that it is OK to express your emotions about the procedure.

3. Remind the child what physical behaviors will be expected, such as holding still, opening the mouth and saying aaah, breathing deeply, etc.

4. Choose distracting or relaxing activities or sources of stimulation: squeezing your hand or a ball, playing a handheld video game, watching a video, deep breathing and relaxation, imaginative involvement, storytelling, and puppet play, to name a few.

5. Practice counting or clocking the amount of time that will be spent in a procedure. (Counting *down* works better than counting *up* the number of minutes or seconds.)

6. Negotiate a reward that is contingent on making a good effort at using coping skills. Then have the child keep the reward in his or her hand or in mind while performing the coping skill.

Using Rewards and Punishment

As previously discussed, painful medical procedures are often mistakenly experienced by children as a punishment for some wrongdoing in the past. Children who feel this way are often confused, upset, and even betrayed by parents and caregivers they trust. For this reason alone, it is counterproductive and unnecessary to use punishment to attempt to control a child's behavior during an invasive procedure.

Occasionally, parents are driven to experiencing feelings of mortification and desperation by children who are terrified and out of control in the pediatrician's office. At such moments, parents may resort to threatening the child with punishment for "misbehavior." Needless to say, by the time this happens, it is too late to get much voluntary cooperation from a child. Often the outcome is that physical force is used to help control the child. This response sends a clear message to the child that he or she has failed to cooperate, and is being punished for "bad" behavior with physical restraint and use of adult force. The procedure gets done and the child is left with a bad feeling of being a passive participant in an unpleasant power play. There are better ways!

Many parents attempt to use bribes to gain a child's cooperation for an invasive procedure. As a parent, perhaps you feel guilty for having to put your child through an ordeal, so you say: "OK, after we're done with the dentist, we'll go to the movies." While the sentiment is nice, this is not an effective way at communicating your specific expectations to a child about how to behave while at the dentist. Others try, "If you behave well and you don't do anything bad, I'll buy you a toy." This may work with some children on occasion, but even when it does, the reward gives no hint to the child as to exactly what is meant by "bad" or "behave." He may try to control himself this time, but he will not learn how to apply the good behavior to other situations.

Positive Reinforcement: Negotiate Ahead of Time

A special type of reward is called *positive reinforcement*. When you wish to help your child achieve a specific behavioral goal, like holding his mouth open, holding his arm still, or practicing a distraction technique, you can negotiate an agreement beforehand that the specific behavior will result in a specific positive consequence, like a prize, a toy, special time with Mom or Dad, or the like. The reward is *contingent* on the agreed upon specific behavior. The child gets a clear set of rules and instructions so that he or she knows exactly what behavior results in what consequence. It is very helpful for the child if he or she gets to select the behavior and reward. In this way, for example, a girl getting a blood test might make a deal with her mother that if she sits down in the chair without delay, she will earn so many stickers for her sticker book. Then, if she can hold still for the needle, she could earn so many more stickers. She is free to decide which behaviors she would like to engage in and therefore how many stickers she would like to earn.

For positive reinforcement to work best, the reward and the behavior should both be specific and simple to understand. It should also be set up in such a way that it is possible to succeed. It is pointless to try to reinforce a behavior that the child is unable to control in the first place. The child will often tell you whether the expectation is realistic. A good rule of thumb is to make sure the child always wins something for trying and something extra for succeeding. Avoid negotiating or changing the rules after the fact. Make sure the target behavior is not too easy. Children are easily insulted if you ask them to cooperate with something that is already very easy for them.

Be prepared for the possibility that sometimes a procedure is just too scary and difficult for the child. A second plan of action should be worked out with the doctor or dentist in advance. If physical restraint is needed, learn to provide it in a nonpunitive way—"This shot is just too hard for you to hold still for, even though you are trying your very best. I'm very happy with how much you've tried, but I can see that you don't think you can hold still without my helping you a bit. That way we can finish this quickly and go home." Notice that the use of physical restraint is introduced as support, not punishment.

Setting Limits During Invasive Procedures: Imposing Just Enough Authority

Up to now, we have shown that respect for children's feelings can reduce their experience of pain, fear, and humiliation. As we have seen, when the child has an adequate understanding of the how's and why's of a painful procedure, he can make better sense of his feelings of distress during and afterward. It is especially important to help children learn a sense of bodily integrity and dignity at a time when they are subjected to taking their clothes off in front of a relative stranger and having their bodily and personal space invaded.

Setting limits is an essential part of parenting a child through any difficult situation. Let's face it, what child in his or her right mind would go through with an immunization unless an adult said that it was not a matter of choice? If the child merely complains, saying, "I don't want a shot," often all that is called for is a firm answer indicating it is not a choice. The difficulty begins when the child resists out of apprehension, fear, or anger. At moments like this, it is easy for parents to forget who is the parent and who is the child. Sometimes the child's fears lead the parent to err in one of the following two directions.

We often "go soft" on the child, resorting to too much explanation and negotiation. This approach does not always allay the child's fears, because it conveys a possibility that the child, and not the adult, is controlling a scary situation.

On the other hand, some parents become a bit too rigid. Out of fear that the child will not cooperate, they may resort to unnecessary threats or intimidation. There are a number of drawbacks to taking an excessively hard line on children at the doctor's office. First, it is premature to use the "heavy artillery" of parental authority before it is definitely needed. When parents become very authoritative early in the game (upon first hearing a child's protest), the child gleans that the parent has already come close to using up all his cards. Children can sense when their caretakers are feeling guilty about inflicting the doctor on them. How? Just as in our description of the "too-soft" approach, children know that when their parents act impatiently, it may indicate that they are losing control and can sometimes be cajoled into giving in.

When you start out with strong resolve to set firm limits, it is not so easy to stick to your guns. Most parents have a natural soft spot for their children when they show fear. In most situations *other* than at the doctor's office, you can play the hero and protect the child. That is exactly what the child expects in the doctor's office, that Mom or Dad will rescue him or her from the scary needle. Tension rises when this does not happen.

A third problem with an overly authoritative approach is that children do not get the chance to learn about their own capacity for self-regulation. How much can the child understand about the situation without being told? How cooperative can the child be without coercion? Can the child ask questions of the doctor by him- or herself? Can he or she hold still for a blood test? What is the smallest possible amount of physical restraint necessary for the child to be able to endure the pain and fear inherent in an immunization?

GOOD LIMIT SETTING

Good limit setting is:	*Good limit setting is not:*
supportive	punitive
controlling	coercive
planned	arbitrary
understandable to children	confusing
confidence-building	humiliating
self-assured	tentative
impersonal/legalistic	individualized

When Adults Invade Children's Personal Space

There is a side of parenting to which adults might hesitate to openly admit. I am referring to the countless times when we knowingly cross the boundaries of a child's physical/personal space, often without his or her consent. The thoughtful caregiver strives to respect a child's physical and emotional integrity at all times. Nevertheless, there are many occasions every day when we physically handle the child's body in order to get some necessary procedure accomplished. These are times when, for better or worse, you "pull rank," that is, exert parental authority over the child when he or she cannot make decisions to act on his or her own behalf. At such times, we often say to ourselves that we are doing such and such "for the child's own good." Examples of this include diapering; dressing and undressing; bathing; giving medicine by mouth, ear, nose, skin, or rectum; taking temperature by ear, mouth, armpit, or rectum; nail and hair care; and examining the child's body for ticks, lice, rashes, or other parasites.

Imagine yourself, if you can, two years old, and in a position of total trust in your father. You are playing happily in the bathtub when father begins to apply shampoo to your scalp. At first it's fun, the lather dripping down into islands on the bathwater. Then, some gets in your eyes. You cry out from the burning sensation, and your sudden inability to see through the suds. Now your father quickens his efforts to rinse your hair, but as you see it, he seems to be doing more to prolong the pain than relieve it. When the soap and the pain are gone, you are (like most two-year-olds) left with a distinct dislike for shampoos. We might go so far as to say that children who have learned to fear soap in the eyes experience pain more severely than children who manage to avoid this problem.

Compared with so-called invasive medical procedures, these might be called "practice procedures." Yet, many parents and child-care workers come to realize that the way we handle these tasks sets the tone and expectations for children's behavior during more invasive procedures like shots.

Even when there is no pain involved, it is easy to see how the child might feel if that caregiver finds it necessary to use physical force. Adults who use force and threats to accomplish brushing of teeth every evening are likely to feel "forced into" using the same or greater force when the child needs a shot. On the other hand, children who have been given the chance to develop more autonomy over procedures like dressing, washing, and haircuts are less likely to require coercion at the doctor's or dentist's office.

Any parent or child-care worker who cares for more than one child at a time, or, who tries to hurry a child through changing, dressing, diapering, or bathing, is sooner or later humbled by children's ability to resist, obstruct, or otherwise frustrate your best efforts. Recent years have seen a heightened awareness of and sensitivity to a child's right to be protected from inhumane physical invasion, punishment, or abuse. Advocates of children's rights have finally begun to protect children who cannot protect themselves from unsanctioned corporal punishment by teachers, child-care workers, and, in some cases, parents. The new climate is causing adults to rethink these coercive situations which have been taken for granted. By safeguarding the dignity and personal integrity of small children, we also sensitize adult caregivers to their power to protect children from unnecessary pain aggravated by fear.

Parents may question whether this is an impossibly utopian picture. What would it take to fulfill this picture? Must we behave like saints and martyrs? The answer to the first question is no, not really. To the second question, no, not at all. What is required is a conscious decision to make the child's emotional welfare a priority, not just at key moments like birthdays and first days of school, but also in between, during bathing and grooming, and routine visits to doctor and dentist. What sets parents and caregivers like this apart is an understanding that children need your attention when they are uncomfortable, and your attention takes you away from adult-oriented thoughts and activities.

In practice, there are a few hints that can help remind us of our obligations to children.

- Leave enough time for routine child-care activities. Avoid rushing.

- Make dressing, grooming, and like activities part of a daily routine.

- Before handling children of any age, tell the child what you are about to do.

- Use your own frustration level as an indicator of the child's vulnerability.

- Allow children reasonable but limited choices whenever possible.

- Involve children in creating ways to ease or avoid their own discomfort.

16

Using Medications

Always consult your physician when you have questions about using any medication for your child. Have a discussion with your pediatrician about his or her philosophy of using medicine for cold and flu symptoms, pain, fever, or any other symptom that might warrant medication. Just because there are a panoply of over-the-counter products available at your fingertips, it does not mean that you should use them indiscriminately. One of the larger purposes of this book is to provide parents and caregivers with the idea that there are many ways of alleviating pain.

Painkillers are among the most widely used prescription and nonprescription drugs. Whether a child hurts from a recent injury, from transient stomach discomfort, or as a result of a chronic illness, the pain does not exist in a vacuum. You can get a very good understanding of the type, severity, and function of a child's pain by looking at your child's pain behavior in context. Remember that, while you cannot see your child's pain per se, you can usually see good evidence from his or her behavior that something is awry.

Behavioral scientists rely very heavily on observed pain behavior when they compare different methods of pain relief. The makers of children's analgesics want to know how quickly Sara's earache will be better after taking the pain reliever. But pharmaceutical companies cannot be satisfied with any one single indicator of Sara's pain. So they observe hundreds of families with two-year-old children, wait for the inevitable earaches, offer one type of pain reliever to one set of caregivers, and another type to a comparison group. Then, behavioral scientists collect as many reliable clues as possible to compare the effectiveness of the two drugs. The results of the comparison might show that one drug reduced the amount of crying, improved sleep, and required fewer doses than another drug.

Comparisons are rarely that cut and dried in the real world. More likely, one painkiller will be more effective in reducing pain but may cause other unwanted side effects like stomach upset. Another analgesic might work very well for earaches, but not as well for headaches. Some painkillers improve the child's emotional outlook but fail to reduce inflammation. Still others are very effective at reducing inflammation but cause severe irritability in many children. Pain behaviors are a vocabulary for parents, caregivers, and scientists to describe and compare different types of pain and different types of pain relief.

So, when you are about to give your child a pain-relieving medication, be it prescribed or over-the-counter, think about what you are trying to accomplish. How much pain behavior and which behaviors do you hope the pill will change? What kind of side effects are you and your children willing to endure? How long are you expecting/willing to wait before getting some pain relief? At what point would you decide that the pill was ineffective and try another approach? When would you consult the pediatrician? What do you intend to do to help the pain reliever accomplish its work?

It is also valuable to know something about how a particular pain reliever is thought to work. Some medicines like aspirin and ibuprofen relieve pain by reducing inflammation around an irritated area. That is, they work "locally" at the part of the body from which the pain originates. Other agents like acetaminophen seem to work more "centrally," or at the level where pain signals are transmitted and received by the brain. Narcotics like codeine and morphine also work centrally, but with a different mechanism than acetaminophen. Narcotic analgesics or opioids block pain signals from being transmitted within the brain, dull their intensity, and create a mild sense of euphoria, leaving the person aware of painful sensations but unconcerned about them. Some analgesics can cause new pain, for example, as aspirin can in the stomach, while at the same time alleviating pain somewhere else in the body. Painkillers can occasionally cause nausea or constipation. Every time you give your child a pill for any ailment, you must balance the benefits produced by the medicine against the costs of the side effects.

Whether the pediatrician has prescribed an analgesic or you bought it over the counter, it is always important to read the label for several key points of information:

Indications. This tells you what kind of pain the medicine is for. Some drugs are marketed specifically for muscle and joint pain; others are for aches associated with cold and flu symptoms or for stomach distress. Still others are for teething and gum pain. Make sure you are using the medication for an indication listed on the label; otherwise you risk not getting any benefit. The medicine shelf at the drug store can be intimidating at first, but if you have an idea of what you need help for, your pharmacist can provide very sound advice.

Dosage. This part of the label tells you how much and how often to take a medicine according to the age or size and weight of your child. Many parents make errors by misreading or misunderstanding dosage instructions. The most common error is to give the child less than the indicated dose. All this does is fail to provide the desired effect and allows the pain to continue unchecked. The longer pain continues, the more upset your child will become, and consequently, the more difficult it will be to "catch up" with the runaway pain. When you give the correct dose of the medication you are trying to "stay ahead of the pain." This means simply that you are preventing it from becoming severe at any time. This avoids unnecessary fear, anxiety, and disappointment in your child.

The second type of mistake many parents make is to wait too long between doses in hopes that the pain will subside by itself. Most dosage schedules suggest taking pills every so many hours, or as directed by the physician, but many parents read this to mean "as needed." The best thing to do is to give a child the pills as frequently as directed, even if the pain has begun to subside. This way, you reduce the risk of "falling behind" the pain and, again, allowing it to run unchecked. A very common consequence of waiting too long is that the pain is allowed to recur with such intensity that any further use of the same analgesic becomes ineffective, even at the recommended dosage.

Administration. This indicates how the drug is administered. Topical or transdermal analgesics are rubbed on the surface of the skin or applied via an adhesive patch and are absorbed into the system that way. Similar modes of administration include rectal suppositories and sublingual pills. Suppositories are absorbed through the mucous membrane along the walls of a child's rectum and are given to babies and toddlers who for whatever reason are unable to ingest medicine by mouth. Oral preparations come in liquid, chewable, and tablet form.

Many parents know that the effort to get a child to swallow a medication can become more of a problem than the condition the medicine was supposed to treat in the first place. It is always preferable to tell your child that he or she is taking medicine and for what reason. Efforts to hide medicine in food often lead to distrust and anxiety over whether the whole dosage was ingested. If your child cannot swallow a pill and it needs to be crushed and mixed with food, make sure you select a food that does not impair the effect of the medication. (Ask your pharmacist or physician.)

If possible, let your child select the food in which to mix the medicine. That way there is a greater chance of cooperation. Some foods I have had success with are ice cream, pudding, apple sauce, and yogurt. Let your child feed it to himself if possible, to minimize any sense of coercion. If pills have to be given every few hours over several days, create a pleasant medicine-taking atmosphere. Make it predictable and ritualized, and help the child understand what the medicine is for. If your child resists, many of the coping techniques mentioned earlier can be used to help children swallow medicine.

Some dos and don'ts for using analgesic medication.

- Do consult your pediatrician before medicating your child.

- Do use the full prescribed dosage for the ailment indicated on the label.

- Avoid "as-needed" dosage of medications. Take as prescribed on the bottle by the clock.

- Do inform your child in simple words what any medication is for.

- Do help the child self-administer whenever possible.

- Do not use placebos. While a placebo may alleviate pain in the short run due to a psychologically expected effect, it ultimately undermines trust, and its benefit soon vanishes.

- Do use analgesic medications in addition to all the psychological methods described in this book. One approach never need replace another.

- Take every opportunity to teach safety in drug use to children.

- Set an example by taking care of your own health with the same empathy and concern you would for a child.

Teaching Toughness vs. Allowing Emotional Expression

Vignette: Sally's Slide

Sally's parents enjoyed the moment when their two-year-old toddler, Sally, had her first solo ride down the slide. She landed with a thud on her backside and looked up expectantly to see her parents' reaction. In one version, Sally looked up at her mother and father with wide eyes and burst into laughter, saying, "Go boom!" In the alternate version, she burst into tears, reaching out to be rescued.

The thrill of sliding sets the child up for an intense emotional experience of some kind. *Which* kind depends on the temperament of the child, on the immediate reaction of the observing adults, and, to some extent, on the impact of the child's landing at the bottom of the slide. What is the best approach for Sally's parents in this situation? There is no simple answer. Sally's world begins and ends with her parents. They have the power to define her emotional experiences as either frightening or exciting, depending on their own predilections. If Sally's parents are sure that Sally is feeling pain from landing on the ground, then they ought to be more ready to offer comfort. If, on the other hand, they are fairly certain that Sally is not in pain, then they might help her to define the experience as fun, cheering, "What a great ride!"

The caregiver who neither minimizes nor overreacts to a child's experiences will help the child discover his world in an envelope of realistic safety. Sometimes it is helpful to let the child take risks, endure the painful consequences, and learn from the experience. Often, however, we decide on behalf of the child that a form of play is too dangerous. As children grow, the parameters and boundaries of risk and danger change continuously. A parent struggles to keep pace with his children's growth so that he can expose them to age-appropriate challenges until the child is on his own.

17

Alternative and Complementary Approaches to Pain

In addition to your pediatrician and your pharmacist, there are a number of other health and wellness practitioners who have a great deal to contribute to the treatment of all kinds of pain and health problems in children. Because health care in the United States is largely dominated by Western allopathic medicine, many complementary and alternative methods of treatment are met with skepticism and even opposition. Nevertheless, society has begun to demand more flexibility from insurance providers, and recently, more and more providers are covering treatment by homeopathic and chiropractic doctors.

While an in-depth treatment of pain treatment with traditional, folk, and homeopathic approaches is beyond the scope of this book, a very brief discussion may help orient you to what is available. Alternative medicine is often meant to be a substitute for Western medicine. Complementary approaches are, by definition, used as an adjunct to modern medicine. It is, perhaps, not appropriate to judge the efficacy of nonmainstream approaches by the same standards as Western medicine. Few alternative approaches have been subjected to rigorous scientific scrutiny, and, with a few exceptions, alternative approaches are unregulated by government or the insurance industry. This leaves the responsibility for selecting a practitioner up to you, the consumer.

In general, it is advisable to check references before seeking the services of any pediatrician, psychologist, chiropractor, homeopath, herbalist, or other health and healing practitioner. If you are not satisfied with the care you or your child is receiving, complain about it, ask questions, get other opinions, or, if all else fails, switch practitioners. Finally, choose a pediatrician who shares your views on health care. Your child will receive better care if you do not need to conceal from the practitioner your adherence to other forms of health care.

Homeopathy and Herbal Medicine

Adherents to homeopathic and herbal medicine approaches may shun popular analgesics like aspirin and acetaminophen in favor of preparations that are thought to activate the body's own internal resources for fighting pain and illness. Homeopathic preparations consist of trace concentrations of substances that, when taken internally or topically, are thought to trigger the body's immune response to irritants such as allergies and infection. These approaches are not simply applied in a vacuum, but rather combined with many of the psychological approaches described in previous sections of this book. For this reason, they are often referred to as "holistic." The goal is to treat the whole child, body, and soul, rather than some specific localized problem in his body.

Herbal medicine has gained wide interest as Western physicians have begun to rediscover the wisdom of indigenous healers from all over the world. Just as with Western medicine, parents should be cautious about offering herbal remedies unless they have been subject to quality control. Otherwise you may not know what dosage your child is receiving, and whether the herbal preparation is pure.

Chiropractic

Practitioners of chiropractic medicine are well respected in many circles of health care and have a devoted clientele. By making mechanical adjustments in the neck, head, and spine, the chiropractor corrects subluxations, improves musculoskeletal alignment, and thereby alleviates pain. Many chiropractors are specially attuned to children's bodies and can help them achieve better posture and even improve athletic performance. A number of chiropractors espouse a combination of herbal and holistic health approaches and can suggest multiple approaches to children's health problems not available from your pediatrician. Chiropractors are not usually used as a substitute for the family doctor. Rather than wait for a pain condition to develop, parents bring their children for adjustments on a regular basis as part of maintaining health and hygiene. If a musculoskeletal pain condition develops, say from an athletic injury or an accident, then special chiropractic techniques are used to alleviate pain and correct any underlying damage done to the skeletal alignment.

Acupuncture/Acupressure

This approach to pain management originated in China over two thousand years ago but has only recently been introduced in the West. Insertion of very thin needles into the skin of patients at strategic points over the surface of the body produces marked relief from acute and chronic pain. The explanation for its effect has to do with the flow of bodily energy called chi and is as yet not well understood by Western scientists. One theory of the effect of acupuncture is that it stimulates the body to secrete its own endogenous painkillers. Acupuncture has begun to gain wider acceptance in the United States as a complementary treatment for a number of chronic ailments in adults; however, it has yet to gain wide use with children.

Acupressure is a type of massage that utilizes many of the same principles that underlie acupuncture. The practitioner applies finger pressure to key points in the body corresponding to chi energy fields, with the result of relieving pain and tension.

Body Work

There are many methods of body adjustment and massage that fall under the rubric of "body work." Each method has its own idiosyncratic theory and its own application for the treatment of pain in children. Examples include Alexander Technique, Zero Balancing, and Rubenfeld Method, to name a few. Some methods combine other modalities such as exercise, meditation, even psychotherapy with the body work. One of the goals of body work is to help the individual become more attuned to the needs of his or her own body; to treat it better, to move with grace and efficiency, and to avoid injury from incorrect use of the muscles and posture.

One of the threads running through the alternative and complementary approaches to pain and healing is that they involve the laying on of hands. There is no doubt that, when used appropriately, human touch is a great analgesic. With the advances in high technology in medicine it has become less and less necessary for the health practitioner to use physical contact for diagnosis or treatment of pain. The physical contact is left largely to you, the parent or caregiver.

Prayer and Meditation

For children as with adults, all pain is both emotional and physical. Alleviate emotional pain and physical pain gets better and vice versa. When a child knows that those around him feel love for him and care for him, his pain will be more tolerable. And if he believes in God, knowing that prayer invokes God's healing can have profound positive effects. If the child knows how to pray or meditate, he can begin to heal himself independently. Prayer generally involves two things: a belief in a higher power and a communal network of believers who support the one who prays. Believe it or not, scientific research has begun to examine the effects of prayer on pain and illness, with early findings suggesting that prayer has an instrumental role in helping people get over illness.

Meditation can help a child learn to quiet the mind, find inner peace, and free him- or herself of some of the emotional and mental stresses that induce or exacerbate children's pain. Children can learn how to meditate and reap great benefit from it. There are scores of approaches to meditation. Some approaches are more physical, and others more mentalistic. Yoga and t'ai chi are physical activities that foster a meditative way of thinking and acting. Both originate in the ancient Far East, and both are easily accessible to children. Movement meditations teach children mastery over the body as well as over mental functions like attention and concentration.

Other meditative methods such as transcendental meditation and Zen generally involve sitting in one place and contemplating sounds, images, ideas, or questions. People who regularly participate in meditation report feeling more rested, alert, free of physical pain or discomfort, and more "at one" with their environment and their surroundings. Children who participate in these activities are likely to be somewhat protected from stress-induced aches and pains. You need not espouse any particular philosophy, religion, or creed to benefit from meditation. In fact, a Harvard physician, Herbert Benson, distilled the essentials of meditation down to a few easy elements that almost anyone can learn, coining the term "relaxation response." He suggested visualizing or saying the number "one" repeatedly with controlled breathing, and relaxed muscles. Adults who do this regularly along with other healthy behaviors show improvements in blood pressure, cholesterol, mood, and overall health. Children stand to gain many of these same benefits.

Involving a Mental Health Professional

Teamwork between the pediatrician and the mental health professional can be crucial in situations where stomach pain is aggravated by both emotional and physical factors. No parent, or child for that matter, likes to hear the doctor insinuate that the pain they are feeling in their gut is in or caused by their head. "Does the doctor think my little girl is crazy?" you might think, or, "Why would my little boy make something like this up?" Unless the pediatrician presents the issue in a thoughtful, nonblaming way, many parents are likely to reject the advice to seek consultation with a psychologist or psychiatric nurse skilled in these areas.

Typically, a pediatrician might examine a child in efforts to diagnose the cause of a recurrent stomach ailment. Failing to find a physical cause, he or she might begin to infer either that the physical causes are undiagnosable, or that there must be emotional or psychological causes for the symptoms. The latter choice is more acceptable to most physicians, whereas the former might be preferable to many patients.

If the physician wishes to refer a child for psychological help, he or she must learn to avoid giving an "all in your head" message. A good referral requires that the pediatrician has a sophisticated understanding of psychosomatic medicine—that is, the aspect of medical care where the mind and the body meet. A savvy parent might ask, "If my pediatrician understands psychosomatic medicine, why, then, does she need to refer my child to a psychologist? Why isn't she equipped to take care of the problem herself?" For one thing, a pediatrician divides his or her time very differently than a psychologist. A pediatrician might see as many as four children in an hour. He or she may be unable to devote the time necessary to understand patients' complex behavioral patterns and then to teach them new ones. A psychologist, on the other hand, might devote as much time as needed for those very problems. (Recent developments in insurance reimbursement have further limited the ability of pediatricians to spend the time necessary to relate on a more personal level with parents and patients.)

The most important element in making a successful referral to a mental health professional is a carefully worded explanation of the reason by the pediatrician. A well-explained referral not only encourages the patient to accept and follow up on the referral but also prepares him or her to benefit from the help provided. Using the vignette about Mike and his referral to Dr. Marcel, an example of a thoughtful referral might run as follows.

Pediatrician: "I asked both of you to come in as Mike's parents even though you are separating and going through a divorce. I wanted to explain to you why I think Mike's stomach cramps keep causing diarrhea, and how you can best help him overcome this problem. You see, Mike's stomach problems are due to a constitutionally vulnerable stomach *and* to the way Mike responds to stressful life situations. The two combined have led Mike into a pattern of missing school and social activities due to stomach symptoms. Now, I have a colleague, Dr. Marcel, who is a psychologist specializing in health problems with emotional contributors. I would like to work together with Dr. Marcel to help Mike. I will continue to help manage his pain and cramps and diarrhea. Dr. Marcel will work with you and Mike to help him manage the stress and emotion-related aspects of his stomach problems. While there are no guarantees, together, we can make progress."

The pediatrician did several things to ensure that Mike's parents would accept the referral. He:

1. involved both parents even though they were getting a divorce

2. recapitulated the physical origins of Mike's stomach problem

3. formulated a psychosomatic explanation using simple, nonblaming language

4. presented Dr. Marcel as a trusted colleague

5. explained the combined roles of pediatrician and child psychologist

6. presented the work as part of, not separate from, Mike's medical care

Now it is the responsibility of Dr. Marcel and Mike to continue to work toward a full understanding of the multiple causes of his condition. Adults and children alike find hope in the statement that there are things that you change through your own actions and things that are beyond your control. Mike may not be able to change his constitution, but he can change the way he responds to stress and stomach pain. If Dr. Marcel is successful, she will help Mike find ways to eliminate avoidant behavior and to make the most out of his everyday life—despite any pain or discomfort he may feel.

Concluding Remarks

The thoughtful parent or caregiver may apply many of the following principles of pain care, outlined in this book, to child care in general.

- Listen to your children.

- Try to understand their thoughts and feelings about themselves.

- Empathize with them.

- Respect their vulnerability as well as their curiosity and bravery.

- Teach them about the workings of the mind and body.

- Select health-care providers who share your beliefs about children's health.

- Advocate for your child, and, if he or she is in pain, take responsibility for getting the pain under adequate control.

Give your child enough information about medical care so that he or she can adequately prepare him- or herself with knowledge and coping skills.

Set an example in the way you care for your own health needs, including pain conditions. Be your child's model for caring for pain. If you are walking around with pain and your children know it, do the same constructive things about it that you would want your children to do. Educate yourself with books as well as by asking your doctor questions about health matters and pain care.

If you ever find your child in the hospital for surgery or any major illness, do not let the medical caregivers neglect managing your child's pain.

Above all, remind yourself, your children, your doctor, and your dentist that *all pain is real*. Be suspicious about a health-care provider who minimizes the complaints of an adult or child without first understanding them fully. If ordinary means of alleviating pain are not effective, seek a doctor's help. Failing that, find a pain specialist. Such specialists can be found in departments of anesthesiology, neurology, psychiatry, and psychology/behavioral medicine in many teaching hospitals.

Suggested Readings

Eisenberg, Arlene, Heidi E. Murkoff, and Sandee E. Hathaway, B.S.N. *What to Expect the First Year* (New York: Workman Publishing, 1989).

Masson, Jeffrey M., and Susan McCarthy. *When Elephants Weep: The Emotional Lives of Animals* (New York: Delacorte Press, 1995).

McGrath, Patricia A., Ph.D. *Pain in Children: Nature, Assessment, and Treatment* (New York, London: The Guilford Press, 1991).

DeSantis, Kenny. *A Dentist's Tools* (New York: Dodd, Mead & Co., 1988).

Stern, Daniel N., M.D. *Diary of a Baby: What Your Child Sees, Feels, and Experiences* (New York: Basic Books, 1990).

Index

About the Author

Kenneth Gorfinkle, Ph.D., is assistant clinical professor of psychology at the College of Physicians and Surgeons at Columbia University. He works with children hospitalized for AIDS, cancer, and heart, brain, lung, and kidney diseases as well as for injuries, drug overdoses, and other conditions. At Sloan-Kettering Cancer Center and at Babies and Children's Hospital at Columbia-Presbyterian Medical Center, he has worked to develop effective methods of understanding and controlling the pain and discomfort that comes with hospitalization for acute and chronic illness.

Dr. Gorfinkle teaches methods of evaluating and treating psychological problems associated with medical illness to psychiatrists, psychologists, pediatricians, surgeons, and nurses. He conducts research on the impact of invasive medical treatment on quality of life for children in cancer treatment. He has coauthored numerous journal articles, pamphlets, and multimedia presentations on the psychological aspects of caring for children with cancer.

Dr. Gorfinkle received his Ph.D. in clinical psychology from the New School for Social Research in 1991. He is married to Doris Ullendorff, a family therapist. They have three children—Gabriel, Naomi, and Margot. Their firstborn, Ari, died after a brief illness in 1988.